LOOK AT MOI PLOISE

Celebrating Aussie life through the decades

LOOK AT MOI PLOISE

BECK FEINER

with Katie Cunningham

murdoch books

Sydney | London

CONTENTS

INTRODUCTION

There are certain moments that have shaped our nation's cultural identity. They may not be the ones we get taught at school, but in many ways, they define our sense of Australian-ness. There's Benita Collings on *Play School* looking at the time on the rocket clock. There's Norman Gunston on the steps of Parliament House, getting in a question as Gough Whitlam is dismissed. There's Scott and Charlene walking down the aisle in *Neighbours*, and there are fashion icons Kath and Kim having a ciggie and a chardy on the patio.

Similarly, no matter where or when you grew up, there are some formative experiences that unite all Australians. It could be watching Bert Newton on TV (in black and white or colour), the sheer thrill of spinning the lazy Susan at the local Chinese restaurant, cheering on our unlikely Olympic speed skating hero 'doing a Bradbury', or learning to swim between the flags and promising to Slip, Slop, Slap.

We think those parts of being Australian are worth celebrating. So from the 1950s to the 2020s, we've collected some of the most unforgettable bits of our pop culture history – inventions, movies, icons, events and the giant statues of fruit that serve as roadside attractions. Not every entry is something to laugh at – over the decades we've had plenty of sombre moments that we'd be remiss not to include. And there's more to the local pop culture canon than we could possibly fit in these pages, so please forgive us if your favourite hasn't got a mention.

Together, the people, moments and creations here paint a picture of our weird and wonderful history. So whether you grew up in Perth or Parramatta, or made Australia your home in more recent times, we hope there's something that tickles your fancy, and possibly has you planning a throwback *Australian Women's Weekly* cake for your next birthday.

The Nifty Fifties

With the Second World War over, the 1950s saw a boom in marriages and babies, and migrants were welcomed as Australians new and old settled into suburban life. We had good reason to stay at home, as television switched on for the first time in 1956 – the same year the Olympics consumed Melbourne. And it didn't take long for us to get a small-screen star in Graham Kennedy, whose variety show, *In Melbourne Tonight*, launched in 1957.

A moreish little biscuit called Shapes came along in this decade, and has remained in our shopping trolleys ever since. In 1959, Qantas began flying internationally, Darwin became a city, Mr Squiggle started doodling, and Australia's population hit ten million.

And Arrernte man Albert Namatjira, a painter who had found fame with his achingly gorgeous landscape paintings throughout the 1930s and '40s, made history when he became the first recorded Aboriginal person in the Northern Territory to be granted full citizenship, at a time when First Nations People shamefully still weren't counted as part of the population.

THE HILLS HOIST

Some of us come from cricketing families; others are raised with the NRL. But there's one game every product of Australian suburbia has played: Goon of Fortune. The rules are simple: peg a cask wine sack to the Hills hoist in your backyard, give it a spin, and whoever the silver pillow stops in front of must suckle from its teat. Repeat.

Shockingly, the Hills hoist wasn't invented to facilitate teenage binge drinking but as a revolutionary new way to dry our washing. Inventor Gilbert Toyne first patented the design for this spider web of galvanised steel back in the 1910s, calling it, simply, Toyne's Rotary Clothes Hoist. But it was Lance Hill and his brother-in-law Harold Ling who marketed the clothesline under the much punchier name of the Hills hoist in the 1940s and claimed most of the glory for its design, going on to manufacture the creations in Adelaide for decades to come. The Hills hoist quickly spread throughout Australian backyards during the baby-booming 1950s, a time when there were seemingly endless nappies to wash and dry. By spinning around and offering easily adjustable height, it promised less physical labour for the long-suffering housewife, making this genius design an instant hit.

But perhaps the most important design feature of all is that the Hills hoist is able to weather even the toughest conditions. As well as never buckling under the weight of the kids determined to use it as a makeshift swing, a Hills hoist was said to be the only thing left standing at the site of one Darwin family's home after Cyclone Tracy tore through.

So when it came time to put together the Sydney 2000 Olympics opening ceremony, the powers that be decided to pay tribute to this Australian icon by including giant roaming Hills hoist robots in the musical spectacular. The goon sack, sadly, didn't make it in.

BERT NEWTON SHOW

BERT NEWTON

You can probably still summon his soothingly melodic voice or picture him on stage, dressed in a trademark tuxedo. You might remember him from the Logie Awards, where he was as much a fixture as the spray tans and champagne. He hosted it no fewer than nineteen times, and won four Gold Logies to boot.

While Bert Newton's career would stretch across nearly seven decades, we first met him in 1954, when he landed a job on the radio at the tender age of fifteen. Before long, with Australians falling hard for the exciting new medium of television, Newton jumped ship and turned to the small screen.

First came a stint on the TV variety series *The Late Show* in 1957, followed by regular appearances on Graham Kennedy's *In Melbourne Tonight*. This was a thrilling new breed of live television – often going out unscripted and unrehearsed – and the comedy chemistry between Kennedy and Newton was immediate and obvious. Then came the musical variety hour *The Bert Newton Show* in 1959. This title was retired a year later but would be revived for a spell in 1975 ... and again in 1989.

Of course, that was all just the beginning for 'Moonface', as he was nicknamed (lovingly, we swear). He was a steady presence, guiding us through so many iterations of television, from the days of black-and-white variety shows to the flashy, big-budget spectacles of the new millennium. Along the way, we'd come to know him for his wry, cheeky approach to Australian history, hosting *20 to 1*, as well as his fourteen-year tenure on *Good Morning Australia*. There, he'd chat to the chef who was whipping up something on stage, or lovingly introduce one of the episode's B-list actors or musicians. At some point, Newton would hand off to advertorial presenter Moira McLean with 'And now, here's Moira' – words that still ring in the ears of any Australian who watched daytime television in the nineties or noughties.

There were ups, downs and the occasional gaffe along the way, but Newton will forever be remembered as a legend of the Australian screen. He died, aged 83, in 2021, farewelled at a state funeral in Melbourne. The Logies would never be the same again.

Mango

AUSSIE ICE-CREAMS

First came the Paddle Pop, in 1953, originally available only in chocolate. In 1955 we got the Hava Heart, a love heart-shaped vanilla ice-cream. Two years later, the Weis Fruito Bar arrived – a blend of pineapple, banana and passion fruit – followed in 1959 by the superior mango version. That same year we got the Golden Gaytime, in all its biscuit-crumbed glory, and not long after came the Splice, a treat so quintessentially Australian that Qantas later began serving them on flights.

It's no coincidence that the 1950s gave us so many of our best-loved desserts. It wasn't until the decade before that home freezers were introduced, a small but revolutionary update. We no longer had to trot off to the corner store for an ice-cream but could now keep them by the boxful at home. Single-serve ice-creams quickly became the taste of Australian summer, a fixture of sweaty December evenings in front of the telly for generations to come. >

There have been evolutions along the way. The Golden Gaytime was originally strawberry; the toffee version we know and love wasn't introduced until the 1970s. The Paddle Pop went on to add a range of flavours, including chocolate-tipped banana (since discontinued but never forgotten) and perennial favourite rainbow (which, in a mind-blowing revelation, is actually just ... caramel?). Weis trialled, and decided against, an all-cream, no-fruit bar. And Streets even ended up consulting with the LGBTIQA+ community on whether they should change the name of the Gaytime: the answer a resounding no.

As for that other iconic ice-cream – the one with a bubblegum nose? While Bubble O'Bill may have been uniquely embraced by Australians – we are the only country, bar New Zealand, where it's still sold – it was first made by an American company in the 1980s. Capitalising on its popularity, homegrown brand Pauls launched a copycat in the image of *Cartoon Connection* host Agro, with his own bubblegum nose. *That* ice-cream is entirely Australia's doing.

'HAPPY LITTLE VEGEMITES'

There are some things you never forget: your childhood home phone number, the recipient of your first kiss, and the 'Happy Little Vegemites' jingle. Aired across five different decades, the tune has been lodged firmly in the brains of generations of Australians, waiting, like a sleeper agent, to be activated at the first sound of that rhyme: *We're happy little Vegemites, as bright as bright can be. We all enjoy our Vegemite for breakfast, lunch and tea!*

The jingle first aired on radio in 1954, and appeared on screen two years later when television finally hit Australia. It has remained a fixture of our ad breaks ever since. Then, in 2023, to mark the spread's 100-year anniversary, Vegemite re-recorded the jingle with a new generation of kids. (Or, more accurately, the *first* generation of kids: a school choir had originally recorded the 1950s jingle, but the advertisement's musical director reportedly hated their performance so much that he replaced them with professional singers imitating children.)

Contrary to the lyrics, we didn't *always* enjoy our Vegemite. When the dark, delicious and oh-so-divisive spread was first introduced in 1923, it struggled to compete with rival yeast extract Marmite. Eventually, after a jar was given away with every Kraft cheese purchase, it won over Australian palates and, by the 1940s, nine out of ten Australian homes had Vegemite in their pantry. (You wouldn't store it in the *fridge*, would you?) As a nation, we've been debating the correct Vegemite-to-butter ratio ever since ... and watching in horror as foreign visitors naïvely apply thick black smears of the stuff to their toast.

Of course, not every subsequent Vegemite endeavour has been as successful – iSnack 2.0, we remember thee. But 'Happy Little Vegemites' still feels like Australia's other national anthem.

LOUIE THE FLY

He's bad, mean and mighty unclean. And he's been spreading disease with the greatest of ease for over six decades now. He's Louie the Fly – star of the enduring Mortein ads, and a true all-Australian villain.

Louie first buzzed onto screens in 1957, only a year after television's official launch in Australia. That very first black-and-white advertisement saw him fly around a sleeping baby, 'afraid of no one but the man with a can of Mortein'. Remarkably, the idea for Louie the Fly came from Bryce Courtenay – who would go on to become the legendary Australian author of books like *The Power of One*, but was then a 24-year-old advertising creative punching the timecard. Courtenay and the voice actor behind Louie decided that the cartoon fly should have a voice like a Chicago gangster, 'but more guttural'. And while the Mortein ads have grown more sophisticated since then, Louie's signature drawl has remained the same. Courtenay, for his part, later expressed dismay that his best-known contribution to Australian culture wasn't his bestselling fiction but a cigar-huffing fly.

Louie wasn't Mortein's only offering to our anti-blowfly defences. By the 1940s, a scientist at the CSIRO had already developed the first personal insect repellent. But it wasn't until 1963, when Queen Elizabeth II visited Australia and was doused in it before an official event, that word began to spread about the magical powers of this new aerosol. Mortein called for the formula and Aerogard was born, leading to the demise (or, at least, temporary delay) of 'the Australian salute' – that second-nature gesture that whacks a blowfly away from your face.

LOCAL MILK BARS

The best among them sold ice-cream spiders, mixed lolly bags, chocolate bars and hamburgers. The bloke behind the counter was probably pulling a twelve-hour shift and his family likely lived upstairs. Your mum might have sent you to grab a loaf of bread or a bottle of milk ... and you may have used some of her money to buy yourself a malted milkshake while you were there.

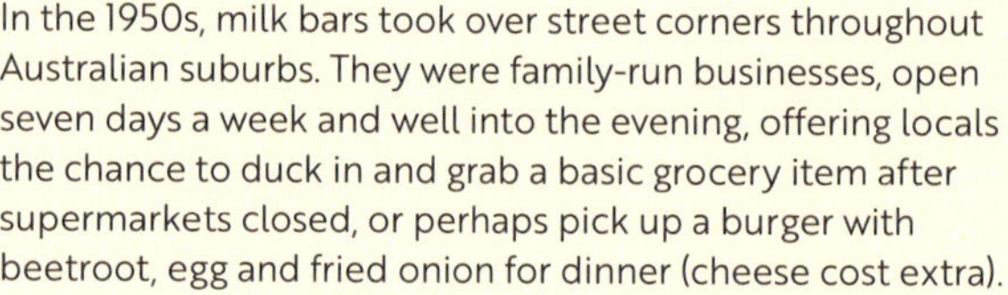

In the 1950s, milk bars took over street corners throughout Australian suburbs. They were family-run businesses, open seven days a week and well into the evening, offering locals the chance to duck in and grab a basic grocery item after supermarkets closed, or perhaps pick up a burger with beetroot, egg and fried onion for dinner (cheese cost extra).

Milk bars were a fixture of the 1950s, '60s and '70s, but they struggled to survive against the onslaught of convenience stores and extended supermarket trading hours. Today, there are just a handful of milk bars, and while their stock may be greatly depleted, those delightfully retro signs remain. For generations of Australians, the magic of what once lay inside those doors will never be forgotten. Fried pineapple ring, anyone?

CREAMING SODA
ORIGINAL
Milk Bar

RIGHT WRONGS
WRITE
YES
9

The Seismic Sixties

In the 1960s, Australia watched as the world underwent big changes. The civil rights movement reached new heights in the US, man walked on the moon, and the Vietnam War escalated, taking Australian troops with it. At home, we converted to decimal currency, succumbed to Beatlemania as four young men from Liverpool toured the country, and lost our innocence as three children in Adelaide, the Beaumonts, went missing – never to return.

We dominated in sport. In the pool, Dawn Fraser won Olympic gold in 1960 and '64, and became the first woman to finish the 100-metre freestyle in under a minute in '62.

On the tennis court, Australia nabbed the Davis Cup seven times throughout the '60s, thanks to greats like Rod Laver. Variety show *Bandstand* kept us glued to the TV all decade long, featuring musical performances from the likes of teenage surf-pop singer Little Pattie, known for tracks like 'He's My Blond Headed Stompie Wompie Real Gone Surfer Boy' (oh, what a song title).

THE 1967 REFERENDUM

Australia has held 45 referendums. Only eight have ever passed. The most important of them happened in 1967.

Nearly 180 years after the arrival of the First Fleet, amid a decade of huge social upheaval, Australians went to the polls to vote on making a small but powerful change. The Constitution, written in 1901, had made just two references to First Nations People: one that gave the Commonwealth power to make 'special laws' for Aboriginal and Torres Strait Islander Peoples, and one that stated they should not be counted in the population. Those 'special laws' led to dispossession of land, control over the lives of Aboriginal and Torres Strait Islander Peoples, and the Stolen Generations of children to name but a few of the consequences. That we didn't even count First Peoples as citizens added insult to injury.

Support for changing the rights of First Nations People had slowly swelled during the 1960s thanks to the work of groups such as the Federal Council for the Advancement of Aborigines and Torres Strait Islanders (FCAATSI), which included prominent Yorta Yorta pastor, sportsman and activist Sir Doug Nicholls. The referendum was spurred in no small part by concerted campaigning by FCAATSI and others, as well as by the likes of South Sea Islander Faith Bandler, and aided further by high-profile protest events like the 1965 Freedom Ride and the Wave Hill Walk-off in 1966. In the lead-up to the referendum, powerful slogans called for equal rights, asking Australians to 'right wrongs, write yes'. They worked. On 27 May, 90.77 per cent of the population voted yes – still the most resounding 'Yes' result we've ever had.

In some ways the 1967 referendum can be considered the beginnings of reconciliation and evidence of the widespread desire for a kinder, more just country. But it was only a small step towards recognition of the ongoing damage done by colonisation.

1967

'WHAT IS IT, SKIP?'

In the late 1960s, a new TV show enraptured Australia and the world. *Skippy the Bush Kangaroo* followed the adventures of Sonny Hammond, the son of a park ranger, and Skippy, the wild kangaroo Sonny had found orphaned as a baby.

And Skippy wasn't just any kangaroo. She could communicate with the Hammond family using her trademark *tchk tchk tchk* (a sound that, we are sorry to tell you, actual kangaroos do not make). She had a finely tuned radar for danger and was able to lend a paw if someone was, say, trapped down a well or being circled by a shark (yes, both of these things happened in *Skippy*). And she was always there to thwart the bad guys, who seemed to keep popping up in Waratah National Park, an apparent hotbed of hijinks and mayhem. She could open doors, start a car, play the piano and fetch the mail. One episode even saw Skippy go to Randwick Racecourse, place a bet on the horses ... and win.

Skippy the Bush Kangaroo became a global hit, screening in 128 countries to an audience of over 300 million each week. In France, it was *Skippy le Kangourou*; in Germany, *Skippy, das Buschkänguruh*. The show's actors were mobbed wherever they went, and young fans would crowd Australian shopping centres for a chance to 'meet and greet' Skippy (or, at least, some other female eastern grey on a leash). The series attracted celebrity guest stars of the era like Frank Thring and pop group The Executives. There were product crossovers like Skippy Cornflakes, and some 70,000 young Australians joined the pre-internet fan club 'The Skippy Club'.

Skippy lasted 91 episodes and one feature-length film. All these years later she remains Australia's most famous kangaroo, and likely our greatest small-screen success ever.

BIG THINGS

Today we have the Big Mosquito, the Big Cane Toad and the Big Bin. There's the Big Potato in Robertson, New South Wales, which is not to be confused with the Big Spud in Sassafras, Tasmania. We have two Big Cherries, plus a third that has since closed. There are literally hundreds of Big Things dotted throughout our highways and small towns, some a little more impressive than others.

But back in 1964, there was pretty much just the Big Banana, pride of Coffs Harbour. Local businessman John Landi wanted an incentive for passing motorists to pull over at his banana stand. Inspired by the Big Pineapple in Hawaii, he decided to borrow the concept, appointing an engineer and builder to make his vision a reality. Construction started in September of 1964 and was finished by Christmas, ready for the holidaying crowds to come.

Lying an impressive 13 metres long, 5 metres high and 2.4 metres wide, the formidable creation was swiftly labelled the world's biggest banana. (And if it's not – what is?!) Even as more and more Big Things popped up in the following decades, the Big Banana has remained a leader in its field, up there with the Opera House in the ranking of Australia's architectural wonders. It's even been immortalised on a one-dollar coin and on two different postage stamps. >

Occupying an unmissable pocket of the Pacific Highway – an unavoidable pitstop on any coastal drive between Sydney and Queensland – the Big Banana has always had a geographic advantage in luring passing road-trippers. But, not one to rest on its laurels, it's evolved over the years into a full fun park experience, complete with laser tag, minigolf, ice skating and waterslides (plus banana splits at the cafe). Not that you *have* to go inside for the quintessential Big Banana experience. What really matters is nabbing a photo in front of that iconic, inedible fruit – even six decades later, no family road trip is complete without it.

SCANDAL AT DERBY DAY

Jean Shrimpton didn't mean to change fashion forever on her visit to Australia. Shrimpton – then the world's highest-paid model – had been enlisted to travel from London to Australia for the Melbourne Spring Racing Carnival in 1965. Sponsoring her visit was a textile manufacturer who wanted the model to promote its new acrylic fabric, rolls of which were sent to London so Shrimpton and her dressmaker could design a wardrobe. But they hadn't sent enough fabric to make a modest mid-calf number so, with a shrug, Shrimpton and her dressmaker decided to end the hemline of the dress a full 10 centimetres above the knee.

Shrimpton was sure that nobody would 'take any notice' of her exposed knees. But when she stepped into the members' lounge at Flemington Racecourse on Derby Day, a hush fell. London designers like Mary Quant may have started making them the year before, but miniskirts certainly hadn't made it to Australia yet. The crowds were shocked not only by the length of her dress but by the scandalous absence of a hat and stockings. Men wolf-whistled, women rolled their eyes and photographers got down on their knees to shoot upwards, a trick employed to make the minidress look even more mini. The next day Shrimpton was front-page news – her outfit eclipsing the results of the actual race – and was criticised by prominent Australians. A global media storm erupted.

Three days later, faced with the threat of losing that sweet sponsorship money, Shrimpton toed the line at the Melbourne Cup in a three-piece suit, stockings and hat. But the proverbial horse had bolted. Thanks to Shrimpton, the miniskirt took off globally; hemlines only crept higher as the decade went on. And at the 1966 Spring Racing Carnival, copycats of Shrimpton's design flooded the field. Now, decades later, anyone who has fought their way through boozed-up crowds to get to the portaloos at the Melbourne Cup will agree that a miniskirt is far from the most uncouth thing you'll see at the Spring Racing Carnival.

PLAY SCHOOL

It gave us Benita, Noni and Don. Teds, both Big and Little. The square, arched and round windows. And the rocket clock – or, if you're a little older, the flower clock. For 49 seasons, 57 years and more than 4500 episodes, *Play School* has enthralled generations of Australian children. It now reigns as the country's longest-running children's show.

It all began on 18 July 1966, when the first episode went to air, live and in black and white. A lot has changed since then, but more has stayed the same. The iconic theme song – promising a bear in there, and a chair as well – has remained more or less intact since day dot. Jemima, Humpty, Big Ted and Little Ted have all been there from the get-go, too. But in more recent years, the show has begun to more accurately reflect *all* of the kids watching it: by casting presenters of all backgrounds and abilities. It's also done a great job of using its segments to educate kids about the vast cultures and histories of First Nations People.

The *Play School* host you remember with unyielding love and affection will depend on your age. Don Spencer began his 30-year hosting run in 1968. Benita Collings joined the cast a year later. John Hamblin and John Waters were both there through the 1970s, while Noni Hazlehurst jumped aboard in 1978 and stayed until 1999. More recently, current hosts Karen Pang and Justine Clarke have been on board since the turn of the millennium. But those long-running presenters weren't the only ones to shape young minds. Across the decades *Play School* has welcomed a who's who of Australian actors – including the likes of Deborah Mailman, Miranda Tapsell, Zindzi Okenyo, Jay Laga'aia and Kiruna Stamell. Together, they arguably did as much to raise generations of Australians as our parents (no offence, Mum and Dad).

And the job wasn't always an easy one. While *Play School* stopped going out live, there is still the time crunch of making five episodes a week. This means that presenters are encouraged to improvise and keep going if they make a mistake. This approach has yielded mixed results. In 2013, arts and craft time went viral after presenter Alex Papps made a contraption rather closely resembling a bong. Accidentally, we're sure.

3:00

AUSSIE BEACH CULTURE

Surf music and movies were all the rage in the 1960s and, along our coastlines, there were big developments in the waves and on the shore.

The first foam surfboards became available in Australia in 1960, making the sport newly accessible. Bernard 'Midget' Farrelly – a pint-sized twenty-year-old from Sydney's Northern Beaches – became a national hero in 1964, when he won the very first World Surfing Championship at Manly Beach. Further south, in Torquay, 1969 saw surfer Doug Warbrick get together with his mate Brian Singer to launch a little brand they named Rip Curl. >

Our new league of surfers weren't the only ones braving deep water. Surf lifesaving clubs had been patrolling our shores since 1907, when the first club of its kind set up shop at Bondi Beach. But in the 1960s the program expanded to launch Nippers, which taught kids how to be safe in the water, and also established Ironman competitions for the strongest surf lifesavers.

Elsewhere on the beach? Stroll the shores and you'd find sunbathers rubbing in oil – this was a time when a tan was, dear God, still considered 'healthy' – and kids sucking dry their Sunnyboy ice blocks, which hit shelves for the first time in 1964. Most noticeable, dotting the shore in every colour and print imaginable, was the bikini, a garment that had once been banned in Australia but was now being embraced by the young and daring.

It wasn't all surfboards and shakas, though. On 17 December 1967, every Australian got the ultimate reminder of how dangerous the ocean can be. On that day, prime minister Harold Holt went for a swim at the remote and unpatrolled Cheviot Beach in Victoria. Conditions were rough and Holt was caught in a rip. He was never seen again. A by-election was held, John Gorton became Australia's new PM, and Holt went down as a cautionary tale about the importance of always swimming between the flags. (Then, in an eyebrow-raising tribute, Holt went on to have a pool named after him in Melbourne. The mind boggles.)

NEW
TANTASTIC
DARK-TANNING
OIL

A CHOCOLATE REVOLUTION

The 1960s brought big changes – in politics, in social mores and, most importantly, in chocolates.

In 1963 Bertie Beetle was launched: a chockie initially sold on shelves but later relegated to showbags (where, at just $2 a pop, the Bertie bag found a cult following for its truly unbeatable value). In 1964, Arnott's changed afternoon tea forever when it created the Tim Tam: two malted biscuits, a chocolate cream filling and a thin chocolate coating. It was, needless to say, a hit and, before long, pioneering Australians were biting off opposite corners of the biscuit and using it as a straw in mugs of tea, dubbing the move a 'Tim Tam Slam'.

The Caramello Koala launched in 1966 (first known as the 'Caramello Bear') and began floating down the river to the tune of Donovan's 'Mellow Yellow' in TV advertisements shortly thereafter. The Freddo Frog was first created in 1930 by the now-defunct MacRobertson's, but was sold to Cadbury in 1967, propelling the amphibian treat to new heights. Significant innovations in confectionary, each and every one.

GAY
RIGHTS

70s

The 'It's Time' Seventies

In the 1970s, the big social changes that had been rumbling abroad truly reached Australia, with mixed results. In '72 Gough Whitlam became our PM ... and three years later we were scandalised as the governor-general dismissed his government, the first and only such case in Australian history. A few hundred kilometres away, in 1978, the Gay Solidarity Group marched down Sydney's Oxford Street to raise awareness of queer life. Homosexuality was still illegal in New South Wales and they were met with violence from the police. It was the very first Mardi Gras.

And to encourage us to be happier, healthier and more active, the Victorian government launched a public health campaign called 'Life. Be In It'.

You may well have caught those TV advertisements during an episode of *Young Talent Time*, the variety program that debuted in '71 and helped launch the careers of performers like Tina Arena and Dannii Minogue. At the movies, *Picnic at Hanging Rock* premiered, taking Australian film to the world stage, and on the radio, Barry Crocker dominated. And, in 1979, friends Gabrielle Carey and Kathy Lette published a book based on their experience as teenagers growing up in Sydney's beachside Sutherland Shire, which they called *Puberty Blues*.

It spawned a movie adaptation and gave us the truly immortal line, 'Rack off, ya fish-face moll'.

OUR LIVVY

Throughout the 1960s and '70s, a fresh-faced blonde singer was making her mark on the airwaves both here and abroad. But despite her presence on the country charts, Olivia Newton-John hailed not from Nashville but from Melbourne.

She had moved to the United Kingdom in pursuit of a music career and found huge success with hits like 'Let Me Be There' in 1973 and 'I Honestly Love You' in 1974. Newton-John was the ultimate girl next door, producing soft, heartfelt love songs.

This all changed at a dinner party hosted by singer Helen Reddy, who'd convinced Newton-John to ditch the UK in favour of the US. On that fateful night, she met a movie producer who offered her the role in a musical he was working on called *Grease*, co-starring John Travolta. The chemistry between the on-screen pair was palpable and *Grease* became the biggest box-office hit of 1978 – and one of the best-loved musicals of all time. When Newton-John uttered the line 'Tell me about it, stud' in the film's final act, it felt like no actor had ever done more with only five words.

Just like Sandy, the character she so delightfully portrayed, Newton-John underwent her own good-girl-gone-bad transformation. Or at least good-girl-grown-up. On her next album cover, *Totally Hot*, she sported all-leather attire and teased hair. *Physical*, in 1981, turned up the heat even more, its title track banned from some radio stations for its suggestive lyrics. Her music and screen success kept coming (who could forget her turn as Kira in *Xanadu*?) and, by the end of her career, Newton-John had become one of Australia's most successful recording artists ever. She was recognised with a damehood and inducted into the ARIA Hall of Fame.

But off screen and backstage, Newton-John fought private battles. In 1992, she was diagnosed with breast cancer. She had treatment, went into remission and kept recording and performing, as well as becoming a strong public advocate for breast cancer research. In 2017, her cancer returned. Newton-John died of the disease, aged 73, in 2022. The Sydney Opera House lit up pink in her memory, and Australians mourned one of our best talents and brightest lights. Oh, Sandy.

COLOUR TV ARRIVES

At midnight on 1 March 1975, television in Australia changed forever. As the clock struck twelve, our TV screens finally burst into colour. 'C-Day', as it was known, had been a long time coming – the high cost of the equipment required for the changeover had delayed its arrival to Australian shores.

And public anticipation of colour telly was high. By 1967, our TV stations were already setting up displays at shopping centres to educate audiences about the exciting new medium, and ads for colour-compatible TV sets had been popping up in newspapers since 1969. In 1972, the Australian government finally set the date for colour conversion, and from October 1974, colour test patterns began appearing on our screens, giving viewers a chance to correctly tune their set. Five months later, it was all systems go. *The Aunty Jack Show* was the first program broadcast in colour – the ABC sneakily ditching black-and-white 30 seconds before midnight to beat the commercial networks.

With our screens now lighting up in brilliant blues, greens, reds and yellows, we could now watch Mr Squiggle doodle the rainbow, as Blackboard implored him to 'Hurry up!' The bold new possibilities of colour television allowed exciting new programs like *Chopper Squad*, which followed the work of a fictional helicopter rescue team from Sydney. We also got to see, in full colour, all the lurid details of the decade's shows. The '70s gave us groundbreaking soapies like *Number 96*, which dared to air sex scenes and nudity, plus scandalous plot lines covering drug use and devil worship (a prime concern of the era). *Prisoner* delved darkly into the world of women's penitentiaries, proving a hit here as well as in the US and UK.

Still, there were limits to our permissiveness. Funnyman Graham Kennedy found himself (temporarily) booted off TV after (sort of) swearing on his variety show. On his very first colour episode, Kennedy imitated a crow, saying 'faaaaaaark' and was hit with a storm of outrage. He was banned from appearing live on TV and radio by the authorities and shortly thereafter resigned – or, perhaps, was given the axe by the Nine Network. Australia may have been ready for colour, but not that much.

NUMBER
96
Tonight at 8.30:
television loses
its virginity!

CHOPPER
SQUAD

PRISONER

we want gough!

It's time.

GOUGH WHITLAM

It was time for improving, time to come together, time to look ahead, time for moving. In 1972, the Australian people were hungry for change and, thanks in no small part to a punchy campaign slogan and song to match, we got it. On 5 December 1972, the Gough Whitlam–led Labor Party was elected, ending 23 years of consecutive rule by the Coalition.

In a feat of effective political campaigning, the need for a new government was boiled down to two words: 'It's Time'. That slogan was emblazoned on T-shirts and badges, and launched across national TV, radio, print and cinema advertisements. And, in a stirring two-minute tune, it was sung by a roll call of influential Australian celebrities: Bert Newton, Little Pattie, Graham Kennedy, Jacki Weaver and Barry Crocker among them.

The slogan worked because it rang true. After the social upheaval of the 1960s, it really was time for a different Australia. And, on Whitlam's part, the work had already begun before 1972. At the 1969 election, the first with Whitlam as leader, the ALP gained eighteen more seats in the lower house – not enough to form a majority and win the election, but enough to start pushing through a series of reforms around cities, schools and hospitals. So when the 1972 election rolled around, the ALP already had three years of proven change under its belt.

Whitlam promised voters universal health care, an end to military conscription and an increase in education funding. He kept his word, and then some. In his three years in government, Whitlam introduced Medibank (Medicare's predecessor) and maternity leave, legislated equal pay for women, increased social housing, made tertiary education free, passed the first Aboriginal Land Rights Act, implemented no-fault divorce and withdrew the last troops from Vietnam – to name just a few seismic changes.

All up, Whitlam enacted 508 bills during his tenure – which ended abruptly on 11 November 1975, when the Labor government was controversially dismissed by Governor-General John Kerr. But the reforms Whitlam passed shaped Australia as we know it. It was time for better days, and Whitlam brought them.

THE WOMEN'S LIB MOVEMENT

Helen Reddy was strolling through a park, wearing a serene smile and corduroy flares, as she delivered a war cry: 'I am strong! I am invincible! I am woman!' It was the video clip for 'I Am Woman', the song that captured the sentiment of women around the globe.

It was 1971 when the Melbourne-born singer-songwriter first penned the knockout track. She was inspired by the women in her family who had survived 'the Depression, world wars and drunken, abusive husbands'. Fuelled by her own experience in the music industry, where she was objectified, demeaned and spoken down to, she was determined to write a song that captured what being a woman was *really* all about. It resonated, becoming a number-one hit that sold over a million copies worldwide.

The timing was no coincidence. In the first half of the 1970s, the women's liberation movement was banging down the door. At the turn of the decade, abortion was still restricted, the contraceptive pill came with a luxury tax, and women were paid 75 per cent of the male wage and restricted from many professions. Now, women around the country were calling bullshit. The first official women's liberation meetings were held in early 1970; that same year Germaine Greer published *The Female Eunuch*, a media fire-starter that brought feminist ideas to new leagues of women. Even greater leagues were exposed to articles on topics like sex, domestic violence and contraception (plus the country's first nude male centrefolds) when *Cleo* magazine launched in 1972, with Ita Buttrose at the helm. And on Saturday, 11 March 1972, the first major Sydney International Women's Day March was held, with protestors demanding equal pay, safe and legal abortion access and free childcare.

Decades on, there's still work to be done – we continue to wait for that free childcare, and equal pay – but Reddy's track remains an adrenaline shot of empowerment. In evidence of its enduring relevance, after Reddy's death in 2020 the song shot back up the charts – a strong, invincible anthem.

THE ABORIGINAL TENT EMBASSY

In the early 1970s, a pair of shameful decisions spurred one of the most potent protests in Australian history. The decade prior, part of the traditional lands of the Yolngu people in Arnhem Land had been sold without consultation to a mining company. The Yolngu fought for years to get their land back, but in 1971 the Northern Territory Supreme Court ruled against them, on the grounds that native title was not part of Australian law. Then, in early 1972, the McMahon government announced that instead of granting First Nations People ownership of their land, they would only lease it to them in 50-year terms, provided they could show it would be put to 'reasonable' use. The government also reserved the right to use the land for mining and forestry.

Both decisions were met with outrage. In response, on 26 January 1972, four First Nations men from Redfern drove to Canberra and set up a beach umbrella on the lawns opposite Parliament House. They called their settlement the Aboriginal Embassy, because if Aboriginal and Torres Strait Islander Peoples weren't going to be treated as Australians by the government, then they needed an embassy in Canberra, just like other foreign powers. By February the protesters had issued a list of demands to the government, and by April, the embassy had grown to eight tents, and kept swelling from there. It garnered international press coverage, earned support from various foreign diplomats and even then-opposition leader Gough Whitlam met with the embassy to discuss their demands.

It was far from smooth sailing. The McMahon government tried to remove the embassy, and police tore down tents in violent clashes with protesters. But while the exact location of the embassy shifted over the years, protesters never backed down. In 1992, twenty years after it first began, the embassy was permanently re-established on the lawns outside Old Parliament House. It's now the longest continuous protest for First Nations' land rights anywhere in the world: a powerful site and symbol of unbroken resistance.

SOVEREIGNTY

NORMAN GUNSTON

He was a TV host ... but not a very good one. He rocked a bad comb-over and had tissue stuck to his face, evidence of where he'd cut himself shaving. He was unprepared, unprofessional and unimpressed by the celebrity status of his guests. He was Norman Gunston, and he remains Australian comedy royalty.

Gunston – the alter ego of comedian and actor Garry McDonald – first appeared on Australian screens in an episode of *The Aunty Jack Show* in 1973, appearing as a rather terrible TV reporter from Wollongong. McDonald eventually parlayed this appearance into *The Norman Gunston Show*, a satirical take on the likes of Letterman. There, the lights may have been brighter but Gunston was no better at the job. Sometimes he'd nab guests for sit-down interviews in his studio, where they'd be offered a Chiko Roll or perhaps mistaken for some other celebrity.

Or he'd simply ambush international stars at press conferences, where – unaware Gunston was an actor very cleverly taking the piss – they were bamboozled by his strange demeanour and sometimes offensive line of questioning. Results varied: Mick Jagger played along but Keith Moon tipped a beer on his head. ('The Gunston Method', as it became known, proved hugely influential, paving the way for satirists like The Chaser and Borat mastermind Sacha Baron Cohen.)

Despite his haplessness, Gunston pulled off some remarkable feats. First, his running joke about being desperate to win a Gold Logie really did win him a Gold Logie – making him the only fictional character to ever nab one. Then, most outrageous of all, he happened to be in Canberra the day of Gough Whitlam's dismissal. While actual journalists clamoured to get a question in on the steps of Parliament House, Norman Gunston was there shoving a mic in the face of Bob Hawke, then the Federal President of the Labor Party. As Gunston prepared to launch a question, Hawke waved him away with the response, 'Oh, it's a bit too serious for that.' Gunston immediately agreed with him.

HOLDEN VS FORD

In the 1970s, there were a few lines that divided all Australians. You were either a Coles family or a Woolies family (or perhaps a Safeway family). You followed the AFL or the NRL. And you drove either a Holden or a Ford. It was red versus blue and we all picked a side.

Both Holden and Ford had parent companies in the US but they were made here in Australia, tailored to Australian conditions. And they won over Aussie drivers. By the 1960s the two brands were dominating local car sales and stoking their rivalry by regularly facing off in the Bathurst 1000, a new competition on the racetrack of Mount Panorama. In the decade that followed they made cars that are now regarded as stone-cold classics. Holden rolled out the Kingswood, Monaro, Torana and, of course, the Commodore. Ford gave us the Falcon in multiple, ever-improving 'generations'.

And then there was the battle of the panel vans. Holden had the Sandman – perhaps better known as the 'Shaggin' Wagons', nicknamed for all the room to, ahem, stretch out in the back – which Ford countered with the less successful Sundowner. Both were lusted after by every young man with a driver's licence and feared by every parent of a teenage girl.

The rivalry between the two car companies made its mark culturally, as well – in the 1999 classic flick *Two Hands*, the good guys drive Holdens while the bad guys drive Fords. In the end, the real threat wasn't the other company but offshore manufacturing. After decades of downturn, Ford stopped Australian manufacturing in 2016 and Holden ceased trading altogether in 2020. But those classic 1970s models fetch prices on second-hand car websites that rival a house deposit, proving our love affair with Holdens and Fords isn't quite done yet.

MARGARET FULTON

Before Maggie Beer, before Stephanie Alexander and Kylie Kwong, there was Margaret Fulton.

At a time when many Australian dinners comprised mostly meat and three soggy veg, Fulton encouraged us to expand our culinary horizons. She opened many Australians' eyes to Italian, French, Greek, Spanish and Chinese cuisines, and popularised cooking with olive oil, which at the time was still sold at the chemist as a medicinal product.

A working single mother, Fulton took on a variety of food-related jobs in the 1950s – from heading up the homewares and kitchen department at David Jones to teaching cooking classes for the visually impaired. She began contributing recipes to *Woman's Day* and later stepped up as the magazine's food editor, a position that allowed her to travel extensively and pick up invaluable tips and tricks about international cuisine. But it was her 1968 debut cookbook – titled, simply, *The Margaret Fulton Cookbook* – that made her a fixture in Australian households throughout the 1970s. The tome has now sold over 1.5 million copies and was the first of more than 25 cookbooks she'd go on to write.

Much of Fulton's charm was that she made cooking accessible. She wasn't a snob; she was an everywoman, practical about the realities of feeding a family every day. If you messed up an egg? Doesn't matter – just cook another one. She loved the simple things, believing that butter should be spread so thick you leave teeth marks when you bite, and once declared that, given the choice, her final meal would be bread, cheese and wine. She rallied against the rise of the celebrity chef in the 2000s, advocated for eating Macca's on occasion, and championed the joy of the dinner party. Fulton died aged 94 in 2019, farewelled as the hero who saved us from blandness.

COUNTDOWN AND THE 1970s MUSIC SCENE

In the charts, on screen and behind the scenes, the 1970s were a formative decade for Australian music.

After having some early success here in the 1960s, a little trio known as the Bee Gees stormed the charts in '71 with 'How Can You Mend a Broken Heart'. (Of course, they were English by birth – but had lived in Australia for just under a decade: enough time for us to claim them as our own.) AC/DC ruptured fans' eardrums with tracks like 'It's a Long Way to the Top (If You Wanna Rock 'n' Roll)', their on-stage madness led by the thrilling new blue-collar rock star Bon Scott. In '76, The Saints busted out of Brisbane and became Australian punk royalty. In '77 The Angels lapped the country off the back of their hit single 'Am I Ever Gonna See Your Face Again'. In '78 Cold Chisel arrived with a scalding track called 'Khe Sanh', Midnight Oil released their first album and singer Michael Hutchence joined a fledgling band called INXS.

Meanwhile, down in Melbourne, an entrepreneurial young man called Michael Gudinski founded the now-legendary Mushroom Records. His early signings included Antipodean acts Skyhooks and Split Enz, both of which would go on to claim number-one singles. Gudinski even started a subsidiary

label to Mushroom focused on punk music. Its very first release was a cover version of 'These Boots Are Made for Walking' by The Boys Next Door – Nick Cave's first band.

As for how you'd discover all this vital new music? Perhaps by tuning into *Countdown* every Sunday night at 6 pm, where host Molly Meldrum helped to introduce this whole new world of exciting sounds to Australian ears, providing a generation of Australians with a musical education.

RAMSAY ST
EXPO 88
SUX

80s

The Fluoro Zinc Eighties

The 1980s brought big moments for Australia, both at home and abroad. On the world stage, Pat Cash won at Wimbledon and *Crocodile Dundee* star Paul Hogan became responsible for Americans asking Australians to chuck 'a shrimp on the barbie' forevermore (never mind the fact that they're called prawns here). At home, the State of Origin kicked off for the first time and the World Expo hit Brisbane in '88, bringing with it some 16 million visitors.

On the small screen, *Home & Away* and *Neighbours* began battling it out for ratings, a puppet called Agro became the star of kids show *Cartoon Connection*, Kylie Mole scowled her way into Australian hearts, and *A Country Practice* devastated us all by killing off beloved farmer Molly.

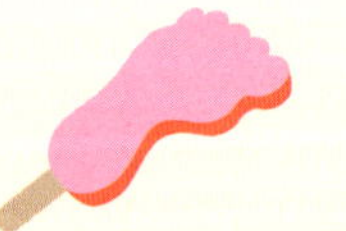

After decades of watching us sizzle in the sun, in 1981 the Cancer Council first asked us to Slip, Slop, Slap, spreading the public health message with the help of a musical seagull mascot named Sid. Elsewhere in our ad breaks, Qantas pulled at our heartstrings with the debut iteration of their commercial 'I Still Call Australia Home'. And we all started waking up early on the weekend to watch *Rage*, a new music video show on the ABC.

We also saw the big-screen breakthrough of a curly-haired redhead called Nicole Kidman, who fought crime on two wheels as part of the *BMX Bandits*. She'd soon decamp to Hollywood, marry Tom Cruise, and swiftly become 'Our Nicole'.

BOB HAWKE

In 1983, Australia claimed an unexpected victory in the America's Cup yacht race, ending the 132-year winning streak of the US. No one was happier about it than prime minister and big-time sports fan Bob Hawke, who immediately declared a public holiday. 'Any boss who sacks anyone for not turning up today is a bum,' he laughed, in words that would quickly become immortal.

Hawke did a lot in his eight-year tenure as PM. He won four consecutive elections, more than any Labor Party leader. He held what is still the highest-ever approval rating for an Australian prime minister, hitting 75 per cent in 1984. He launched the environmental protection agency Landcare, brought in superannuation and, sick of our sporting teams singing the same song as England's, even changed the national anthem to 'Advance Australia Fair'. But we loved him most for moments like this – off the cuff, unfiltered and totally true blue.

After a long history in the trade unions and the ALP but just a few years in parliament, Bob Hawke was elected prime minister in 1983 in a landslide victory. (Not his first or perhaps even greatest achievement – in his university days Hawke famously claimed to have broken the world record for sculling a yard glass of beer in eleven seconds.) He was always a different sort of politician. Yes, Hawke was a boozehound and a womaniser. But he was also uniquely charismatic, down-to-earth and a true man of the people, who rode in the front seat, next to his driver, and insisted he be called 'Bob'. He was warts-and-all honest about his struggles – before the election he vowed to stay sober during his time in parliament – and it only endeared him to us more. He also rocked a pair of budgie smugglers like no other (sorry, Tony Abbott).

Hawke stayed in power until 1991, when Paul Keating toppled him in a leadership spill. In retirement, he went back to the schooners – going viral, at age 83, for sculling a beer 'for the country' during a cricket match at the SCG – though reportedly in greater moderation than before. (Moderation is, perhaps, a relative term here.) He died, aged 89, in 2019, going out as an Australian leader who is often imitated but never bettered.

THE AUSTRALIAN WOMEN'S WEEKLY BIRTHDAY CAKES

There was a piano, a helicopter, a racing car, a rocket. There was the choo-choo train – a feat of engineering so marvellous it made the cover – and the duck, complete with a pair of crinkle-cut chips as a beak (which you may have seen in an episode of *Bluey*). And who could forget the swimming pool, which ingeniously combined jelly *and* cake, plus a delicate little musk stick and liquorice ladder?

If you went to a kid's birthday party in the 1980s or 1990s, odds are you ate something lifted from the pages of *The Australian Women's Weekly Children's Birthday Cake Book* (that's AWWCBCB for, er, short?). This hallowed tome contained 108 recipes for wacky, wonderful and downright inspired cakes, covering off just about any design idea a tiny human could dream up for their big day. It became a staple of Australian kitchens, each recipe an Everest every home cook was determined to conquer. >

What the cake looked like was far more important than how it tasted – in fact, every recipe called for the use of cake mix and a simple cream icing. Not that opting for cake mix made these cakes easy. Sure, some were relatively achievable – like the Smarties-covered cake in the shape of the number one, a mainstay of first birthday parties around the country. But others broke the spirit of just about any who attempted them. Even the cookbook's author, Pamela Clark, advises to steer well clear of the tip truck cake. 'Bitch of a cake – don't make it,' she once told the ABC. 'Glue the pages together – forget it.' In fact, the *Women's Weekly* test kitchen had a dedicated phone helpline for parents experiencing a breakdown as they baked, and, Clark says, it rang off the hook.

Labour intensive though its creations may have been, we never stopped baking. The cookbook was first published in 1980 and sold over a million copies – despite a long period when it was out of print. In 2011, twigging to the demand for its wonderfully kitsch creations, the *Women's Weekly* republished a special vintage edition that looks just like the first one. Minus the dirty little fingerprints, of course.

KYLIE MINOGUE

Before she became the Princess of Pop, Kylie was Charlene, a hot-tempered teenager just trying to make her way as a mechanic on Ramsay Street.

Almost as quickly as Charlene was introduced to the cast of *Neighbours* in 1986 – Minogue's breakout role at age eighteen – she fell hard for Scott Robinson and his shaggy blond mullet. The pair swiftly became the heart and soul of the soapie, reviving its flagging ratings, which were helped along by rumours of Kylie and co-star Jason Donovan's real-life romance. But when a plot line about the young unwed couple moving in together proved a little too progressive for the early '80s, producers decided to marry the pair. And, with that, TV history was made. Two million Australians and 20 million Brits tuned in to Scott and Charlene's wedding, each of us wiping away a small tear as Charlene ditched the King Gee overalls in favour of the biggest, puffiest wedding-dress meringue the '80s could offer up.

That 'I do' was just the beginning of Kylie's career. Within a month of the TV nuptials, her debut single, 'Locomotion', was released, hitting number one on charts around the world. Pop ascendancy underway, she left *Neighbours* in 1988. In the years that followed we watched Kylie don the gold hot pants for 'Spinning Around', delighted at her cameo as the cutest ever absinthe fairy in *Moulin Rouge*, and cheered as she picked up a Grammy for sleeper hit 'Padam Padam' at age 55. Along the way she became a bona fide gay icon and a fashion favourite.

But Kylie never forgot about Charlene. When *Neighbours* filmed what was meant to be its final ever episode, after 37 years on air – after it was axed by Channel Ten, and before Amazon revived it a year later – Kylie returned to reprise her iconic role. She was still married to Jason, still feisty, and this time wearing a denim jumpsuit ... a slightly dressier version of those old overalls, given she was there to attend Toadie's latest wedding.

MATCH

PERFECT MATCH

In a time before Tinder, if you were looking for love, you turned to *Perfect Match*. At 5.30 pm on weekdays, Australians would tune in to Channel Ten to watch hopeful singles step up on stage in search of romance. It was a delightfully innocent dating show. A contestant would ask three potential suitors – all hidden behind a screen – a series of compatibility questions, looking for their 'perfect match'. They weren't given much info to go on. The men were introduced simply as firefighters who wanted to climb Mount Everest or electricians who could waterski barefoot; the women were Geminis who worked as secretaries or perhaps art students who would have liked to be queens.

In the hope that love (or, at least, quality television) would bloom, the contestant and their selected match (and a film crew) would then be whisked away on an all-expenses-paid weekend to a noted romantic hotspot such as the Gold Coast or Coffs Harbour, returning in a later episode to explain how it went. It was hosted by Greg Evans (and, for a two-year stint, Cameron Daddo), who'd do his darndest to insert innuendo everywhere he could and flirt with the show's hostess (a role variously filled by Debbie Newsome, Tiffany Lamb and Kerrie Friend). Completing the cast was Dexter, a 'robot' who would run the 'statistics' on how compatible the couples really were. This all took place on a perfectly '80s pink and purple set, which was adorned with giant plastic love hearts and was sound-tracked by woozy saxophones.

Perfect Match ran from 1983 to 1989, creating at least eleven marriages and many more utter disasters. But long after cameras stopped rolling, host Greg Evans still had the love bug. Perhaps addicted to sealing perfect matches, Evans, after his TV career ended, went on to become a wedding celebrant. Yes, really.

MOUSTACHES OF AUSSIE CRICKET

For the better part of the 1980s, Australia's cricket performance hadn't exactly been red hot. That all changed in '89, when we finally reclaimed the Ashes from England.

The winning squad was united by two things: impressive talent and even more formidable moustaches. Batsman David Boon's was a thick and manicured 'chevron'. Wicketkeeper Rod Marsh's was a shaggier and more unkempt 'walrus'. Captain Allan Border had a mo' of his own, even if it was a little thinner than those of his teammates. And then there was Merv Hughes's 'handlebar', the most fearsome of them all, which reached all the way down to the bottom of his chin and only fanned out larger as it went. Together, this team began a sixteen-year Ashes winning streak and ushered in the 'golden era' of Australian cricket in the 1990s.

Is it a coincidence that our fortunes changed as our upper lips grew more hirsute? Hughes doesn't think so. 'I feel facial hair brings the best out of the players,' he told reporters in 2013, offering some sage advice in the wake of an Australian test loss to India. There may be something to the power of that mighty facial hair. After all, how could the other team *not* feel a little rattled staring down a fast ball from Hughes as *that* handlebar flapped in the wind?

For many years, legend had it that Merv's mo' was insured for $380,000 – and while the man himself eventually quashed that rumour, many Australians would argue it's actually worth a full million. (And, yes, Hughes is still rocking his signature facial hair today.)

Handlebar

Chevron

Walrus

Mo' of his Own

LINDY CHAMBERLAIN

In 1980, five words resounded around the world: 'A dingo's got my baby!'

A camping trip to Uluṟu made Lindy Chamberlain a household name for the worst possible reasons. Under the cover of darkness, a dingo had taken her infant, Azaria, from their tent; Chamberlain let out her famous cry as she saw the animal dart away. It should have been an open-and-shut case – and it was, at first. The initial coroner's inquest into Azaria's death unequivocally found a dingo responsible. But the presiding magistrate was also critical of Northern Territory police in his findings – and the cops, perhaps in response, pushed on with their investigations and posited that Chamberlain had killed her daughter. In a second inquest, they put forth an implausible theory of events, no real motive and only circumstantial evidence. It didn't matter – a Supreme Court jury found Chamberlain guilty, sentencing her to life in prison.

Outside, it was a media circus. Chamberlain had already been convicted in the court of public opinion for not acting as emotionally as a grieving mother 'should', for being a member of the little-understood religion the Seventh Day Adventists, and for the crime of dressing her daughter in black. Outlandish rumours that the name Azaria meant 'Sacrifice in the Wilderness' spread like wildfire and locals paraded out the front of the Darwin court protesting the innocence of ... the dingo.

Chamberlain would serve three years in prison before Azaria's jacket was found in a dingo's lair, prompting her release (and substantial hefty compensation). But she wouldn't definitively clear her name until 2012, when a final inquest again conclusively found that a dingo had, of course, taken her baby.

And the case's cultural impact couldn't be undone. Chamberlain's story would be mined for comedy by everyone from *Seinfeld* to *The Simpsons*; it would be turned into an opera called *Lindy*; and would become the one thing every American knew about Australia (at least, until *Crocodile Dundee* came along). Chamberlain would even be played by Meryl Streep in the 1988 film *Evil Angels*; Streep won an Oscar for her dubious Australian accent. That movie, at least, believed in Chamberlain's innocence.

JOHN FARNHAM

By the end of 1986, there was one song blasting out of every radio and cassette tape: 'You're the Voice' by John Farnham. But its road to the top of the charts wasn't an easy one.

When 'You're the Voice' made its way to Farnham, he was at a low point in his career. Johnny Farnham, as he was initially known, had first broken through with a wince-worthy 1967 track called 'Sadie (the Cleaning Lady)'. By the '80s, however, he'd lost his record deal and was widely regarded as a has-been. So when Chris Thompson, one of the songwriters behind 'You're the Voice', heard that Farnham wanted the song, his answer was unequivocal: 'You've got to be joking. He's not doing it.'

But Farnham was deadset on it. He was deep in debt and knew he needed a big hit to claw his way out and turn his career around. So he recorded a demo of the song in the basement of his home, with the inspired addition of a bagpipe solo. Thompson was won over, but record labels weren't, each one passing on it. The song was shopped around to radio stations without Farnsy's name on it, just so they would consider it. But through sheer persistence, Farnham and his manager Glenn Wheatley eventually built the song's momentum ... and then watched it become a global hit. Over a month after its release, 'You're the Voice' reached number one everywhere from Sydney to Stockholm. The comeback LP that would follow it, *Whispering Jack*, is still the highest-selling Australian album of all time. Farnham's career launched into the stratosphere.

He'd go on to release other hit albums, including *Age of Reason* and *Chain Reaction*, and would scoop up more ARIA Awards than any other act in history. In a mark of his impact, Farnham was even named Australian of the Year in 1987. And while most big homegrown musicians eventually decamp to the UK or US, Farnsy happily stayed put, pooh-poohing the idea of a life in America. We love him for a lot of things, but especially for that.

YOU'RE
THE
VOICE

MARGARET & DAVID

Forget Myers–Briggs or star signs. The true personality test for Australians in the '80s, '90s and 2000s was simple: are you a Margaret or a David?

It was 1986 when *The Movie Show* first flickered onto our screens, with film critics Margaret Pomeranz and David Stratton reviewing the week's new releases. Their armchairs might have been inches apart but their opinions on movies were often separated by an unbreachable divide. Margaret was a woman of the people, not averse to a well-crafted rom-com, a loud pair of earrings or throwing her head back to laugh. David, however, was prim, harder to impress and prone to statements like 'This film makes me embarrassed to be a member of the human race' (this particular pearler in response to J.Lo's 2004 box-office smash *Shall We Dance*). They were each frequently – but lovingly – exasperated by the other's interpretation of films (and, perhaps, life at large). Together, they were pure magic, and their disagreements were a key part of the charm.

In fact, across their entire 28-year run, there were only eleven films Margaret and David both gave five stars to, among them local greats like *The Piano*, *Lantana*, *Samson & Delilah* and *Return Home* – a Ben Mendo vehicle from 1990 largely lost to the sands of time. As for what they disagreed on? Margaret loved *The Castle*; David wasn't so sure. David refused to rate *Romper Stomper*, the Russell Crowe film about a gang of neo-Nazis in Melbourne, because of its violence; Margaret thought it a masterpiece.

The Movie Show ran until 2004, at which point Margs and Dave decamped for the ABC. Their new show, reborn as *At the Movies*, stayed on for another decade, until the pair decided to call time. A mega 700,000 viewers tuned in to their swansong episode, which ended with the ultimate odd couple walking off stage hand in hand. Both ABC and SBS would try to launch other movie review shows, but none could hit that sweet spot – Margaret and David's chemistry was singular. Five stars to them both.

1980s FASHION

The shoulders were puffy, the denim was double, and the hair achieved a volume not seen outside an episode of *Jersey Shore* since. On our noses was a smear of fluoro zinc; in our bike wheels a noisy collection of brightly coloured beads (they were called Spokey Dokeys, and they *ruled*). Eighties fashion really was a sight to behold – and Australia made its own special contributions to it.

Some 16,000 kilometres from the catwalks of Milan, Melbourne gave us Coogi jumpers, those blinding knits that combined just about every colour in the wheel at once. Also in the chunky-knit category – a crowded field in the '80s – was a koala jumper from designer Jenny Kee, worn by none other than Princess Diana when she was pregnant. And then there was artist Ken Done, who began printing his rainbow-hued images of Australian landmarks on T-shirts and jumpers (plus bedspreads, placemats and just about anything else he could think of). What a time.

ZINC
ZINC
ZINC

TWIST
19
PRICE IS RIGHT
1 LUGGAGE
2 WASHER
3
4 SAUNA
5 WAVERUNNER

90s

The Naughty Nineties

Have you ever, ever felt like this? In the 1990s, we all went *Round the Twist* at a lighthouse where strange things happened. Elsewhere on the small screen, Larry Emdur revived *The Price Is Right*, the ABC gave us a much-loved but short-lived music show called *Recovery*, hosted by Dylan Lewis, and every ad break made us feel like Chicken Tonight. And then there were the moments that rocked us. We witnessed tragedy in Port Arthur in 1996, and amazement in Thredbo as Stuart Diver was spectacularly rescued from the rubble after 65 hours, becoming the sole survivor of the 1997 landslide.

In politics, Pauline Hanson asked us to 'please explain' and we got a feisty new PM in Paul Keating, who famously told opposition leader John Hewson he wouldn't call an early election because, and we quote, 'I want to do you slowly'. On the footy field, Nicky Winmar lifted his jersey and pointed at his skin, shouting, 'I'm black and I'm proud to be black', and on the cricket field, the Australian team became the best in the world. A new national radio station was launched, triple j, which had previously been Sydney-only. And the song you couldn't escape all decade long? Daryl Braithwaite's 'The Horses', which became *the* tune every drunk bloke wanted to bellow out at karaoke. (Still is, actually.)

SHANE WARNE

He was the king of spin, the earl of twirl, the Murali of Melbourne. He was Warnie, and he was ours.

Shane Warne redefined what it means to be a sportsman. That is, he sold the great Australian dream that you can be an elite athlete and still enjoy a diet comprising mostly foods sold at the servo. And he sure was elite – Warne was a once-in-a-generation cricketer who took more than 700 test wickets across his career. His finest moments include a delivery so spectacular it was dubbed the 'Ball of the Century', the unbelievable hat-trick he bagged in the '94 Boxing Day test, and saving the day in 2001 when Australia crumbled against New Zealand by nabbing 99 runs – a better score than any of the team's higher-order batsmen.

But what made him such a hero wasn't just that he was one of the greatest to ever don the baggy green. It was *him*: a man who perpetually had a beer in one hand and a durry in the other, yet somehow still convinced Liz Hurley to say yes to marrying him. It was him, strutting onto the pitch with thick white zinc smeared across his lips, or in the commentary box with his mouth wrapped around an entire schooner glass. It was him, in those hair regrowth ads (which were eventually branded as misleading by the advertising watchdog). It was him, telling a reporter that actually, hot chips are a very good pre-game fuel because they make him happy, and when he's happy, he bowls well.

When it came time to say goodbye, after Warne's all-too-soon passing from a heart attack in 2022, Australia knew what to do: we decorated the Warnie statue that sits outside the MCG with can after can of VB. He would've loved it.

BIG DAY OUT

You came of age a couple of times in the Australia of yesteryear. One was when you turned eighteen, the other was when you went to your first Big Day Out.

The festival grew into a rite of passage for music fans, but the Big Day Out all began because promoters Ken West and Vivian Lees wanted a support act for the Violent Femmes, who they were bringing out to Australia back in 1992. In a career-making stroke of luck, another promoter, Stephen Pavlovic, had locked in the debut Australian tour from Nirvana, right before they would release their breakthrough album *Nevermind* and become world famous. Nirvana agreed to add another show supporting the Femmes, and this incredible double-header grew into a 21-act line-up playing over one day in Sydney – all for a $40 ticket. On the bill in '92 were locals like You Am I and Sound Unlimited Posse, and Yothu Yindi, who were riding high off the success of their urgent hit 'Treaty'.

In '93, the Big Day Out returned, this time expanding to Melbourne, Adelaide and Perth, becoming Australia's first annual touring festival and an unmissable summer event that paved the way for countless successors. In the years that followed, the festival would keep attracting superstar international acts, while also becoming a staging ground for the who's who of Australian music. Powderfinger first took the stage in 1994 and came back a further six times; The Living End, Spiderbait and cult Melbourne act TISM also became line-up mainstays. A teenaged Silverchair played in 1995, with Daniel Johns reportedly chased backstage by Hole frontwoman Courtney Love, who thought the young shaggy blond resembled her late husband. The mid '90s also saw repeat appearances from Itch-E and Scratch-E, the electronic duo who famously thanked 'all of Sydney's ecstasy dealers' when picking up an ARIA Award for Best Dance Release.

There would be controversy, tragedy and near bankruptcy by the time the BDO ended its 22-year run, in 2014. But through highs and lows, and no matter who was on the bill, one thing remained the same: whatever city you were in, it was invariably held on the sweatiest, most blistering day of the year. God, it was hot.

HEY HEY IT'S SATURDAY

'Dad reckons there's only one show better than *Hey Hey it's Saturday* and that's *The Best of Hey Hey it's Saturday*,' said Dale Kerrigan in *The Castle*, a statement that captured widespread Australian opinion in the 1990s. For 28 years and more than 500 episodes, *Hey Hey it's Saturday* was a TV juggernaut, bringing absurdity, humour and a couple of giant birds to our weekends.

In the hosting role, for the show's entire run, was Daryl Somers, master of the double entendre, who was joined until '94 by his trusty sidekick Ossie Ostrich. Somers oversaw a freewheeling mix of sketches, talent contests, music, chat, ad-libbed jokes and recurring pranks. The show's exact make-up evolved many times over the years, but across its run *Hey Hey* gave us segments like What Cheeses Me Off (where viewers could air their petty grievances), and Chook Lotto (in which a bunch of numbered frozen chickens were spun in a giant metal cage – incredible, nonsensical). And, of course, there was twisted talent quest Red Faces, in which former Skyhooks lead guitarist Red Symons invariably gave everyone a two out of ten and swiftly gonged them off. Tune in on any given week and you might see Molly Meldrum being done in by a practical joke from Dickie Knee, or Wilbur Wilde singing the Plucka Duck theme song. (How's that for a sentence that would be completely unintelligible to anyone who grew up outside Australia?)

While it would return in later years for the occasional special, *Hey Hey* officially called time in November 1999. There were scandals along the way – and plenty of bits that, in the rear-view mirror, don't look so great – but *Hey Hey* will always be legendary Aussie TV. In the words of Darryl Kerrigan: 'Gong him, Red.'

THE *MABO* DECISION

On 3 June 1992, Australian land law changed forever when the High Court recognised that a group of Torres Strait Islanders held ownership of the island of Mer. With that, *terra nullius* – the concept that Australia was 'nobody's land' before the British arrived – was abolished, along with the legal rationale which had long been used to deny First Nations People any claim to their land.

Mabo, as the case became known, was a true Australian underdog story of right triumphing over wrong. Over a period of ten years, 33 Meriam people, led by Eddie Koiki Mabo, had fought the battle for legal ownership of their land, presenting evidence that the Dauer, Waier and Mer people had occupied the island for hundreds of years. Their victory not only assured their right to occupy the island but also ushered in the *Native Title Act*, which passed through parliament the following year, recognising the essential truth that First Nations People have rights to their land. As prime minister Paul Keating described it in parliament, 'The *Mabo* case ended the pernicious legal deceit of *terra nullius* for all of Australia – and for all time.'

More symbolically, the *Mabo* case was also vital recognition of the connection since time immemorial between Aboriginal and Torres Strait Islander Peoples and their lands, waters and skies. Sadly, of those that were directly involved in the case, three of the plaintiffs – Sam Passi, Celuia Mapo Salee and Eddie Koiki Mabo himself – died before the decision was handed down. Nevertheless, their impact lives forever on: today, native title has been recognised over more than one million square kilometres of Australian land and water.

In practice, native title has proved challenging for many Aboriginal and Torres Strait Islander applicants given the onus to demonstrate a continuous system of law and custom handed down from generation to generation – extremely difficult in many cases given the rapid onslaught of colonisation and its subsequent impacts. And the granting of a native title claim does not mean exclusive land rights are established. In fact, native title rights are superseded by the rights of the Federal Government, mining companies and private owners in instances where there is conflict.

MABO

LEE LIN CHIN

In 1987, an icon appeared on our screens for the first time. After an early media career in Singapore and a stint working as a Chinese-language translator here in Australia, Lee Lin Chin made the move to SBS World News. She'd stay behind that hallowed desk for the next 31 years.

Chin became a hero for multiple reasons. She was a reassuring presence in the lives of generations of Australians. In a very white TV landscape, she was a rare glimmer of Asian representation. And she was a skilled and unflappable presenter, whether she was reporting on horrific global conflicts or being caught out in an unexpected cross back to the studio. Case in point: in 2010, as a rather dashing journalist delivered a terribly serious report from Afghanistan, Chin was broadcast live wondering aloud, 'Who is that handsome –' as the camera cut to the news desk. Like a boss, she didn't miss a beat, pressing on as if nothing had happened. (The clip, however, went viral – and we implore you to go google it.)

Chin brought a little fabulousness to the nightly news. Where other news presenters typically wore plain suits so as not to distract the viewer, she rocked the most daring of 'fits – it wasn't unusual to see Chin in a bowtie and waistcoat, a dress made entirely of plastic, a safari power suit, a shirt with approximately six collars or perhaps some kind of netting draped over her upper half.

Towards the end of her SBS tenure, Chin would lean into her icon status by appearing in self-parodying comedy skits on SBS program, *The Feed*, penning a very sardonic life-advice book and lending her name to a wry Twitter account, ghostwritten by comedian Chris Leben. ('I'm going to the Logies tonight,' one Tweet read. 'Which one of the *Home & Away* boys is most likely to put out?')

In 2018, Chin hung up her news hat. Her reason for departing? Partly a disagreement with SBS management, partly lifestyle. 'Working two days a week didn't give me enough time to devote to the pub and re-reading the complete works of Shakespeare,' she said. 'So now that I work zero days that issue has been addressed.' Queen.

AUSSIE BOX-OFFICE CLASSICS

In the 1990s, Australian cinema took us to the Red Centre, the High Court and ... er, Porpoise Spit. As our film industry began to secure international financing, bigger budgets helped local productions level up. The decade gave us serious fare like *Shine*; controversy-stoking flicks in the form of *The Boys* (based on the Anita Cobby case); and the film debut of a young Sydney director called Baz Luhrmann, *Strictly Ballroom* (a global hit that raked in $80 million at the box office). But what we really did best were those quintessentially quirky comedies.

First came 1994's *The Adventures of Priscilla, Queen of the Desert*, a fish-out-of-water tale about drag queens on a journey across the Australian outback, determined to reach Kings Canyon and put 'a cock in a frock on a rock'. Hugo Weaving, Guy Pearce and Terence Stamp won hearts as they drove a fabulous tour bus through towns like Broken Hill; the costume team won an Oscar for their efforts; and the movie became an enduring LGBTIQA+ classic. (Fun fact: another Australian icon, an uncredited Margaret Pomeranz, appears as the mum of Guy Pearce's Adam.) >

1994 was a boom year for going to the movies – just a couple of weeks later, cinemas screened *Muriel's Wedding*, and we watched as ABBA-worshipping Muriel strived to get married and leave her dead-end town – contending with mean girls Tania, Nicole, Cheryl and Janine along the way. Muriel may have been 'terrible', but the movie was a hit that launched the careers of both Toni Collette and Rachel Griffiths (who was excellent as Muriel's sassy bestie, Rhonda, wonderfully telling Tania she'd 'rather swallow razor blades' than hang out with her).

And then, in '97, along came the Kerrigans, who rewrote the Australian lexicon forevermore. *The Castle* taught us that it's not a house, it's a home; that a conveyancer is not quite the same thing as a lawyer; that it's justice, it's law, it's the vibe; and that if you're listing jousting sticks in the *Trading Post* for $450, ya dreamin'. Straight to the pool room with each and every one of those '90s classics.

1990s SHOUT-OUT

VIDEO RENTAL STORES

Your local may have been Video Ezy, Civic Video, Blockbuster or perhaps one of the smaller chains with names like Video City, Movies 4U or Network Video. Whatever the establishment, the video store was the place to be on a Friday evening in the 1990s, and video night was a ritual faithfully observed around the country.

First, you'd make a dash for the new releases ... and find that all twenty copies of the title you really wanted were already on loan. So you'd stroll the aisles for approximately an hour looking for something else that hit the sweet spot, scrupulously averting your eyes as you passed the 'adult' section but stopping to take a good look at all the freaky horror movie covers.

Once you'd settled on a stack of videos, you'd whip out your laminated rental card, head home and sometimes find that the wrong tape had been put in the box. Then it was time to fast-forward through the movie classification ads, microwave some popcorn and settle in. Later you'd probably be fined for not returning the video on time ... or, perhaps, forgetting to rewind the tape. It was *awesome*.

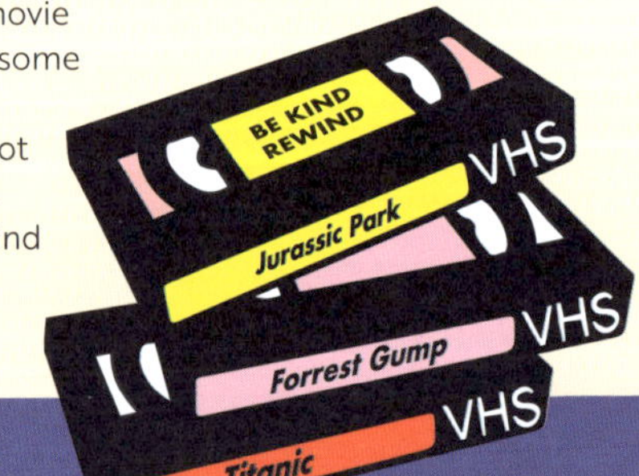

VIDEO
Land

RETURNS

KEVIN
07

NOT HAPPY, JAN!

The 'Not happy, Jan' Noughties

We all started the new millennium bracing for the Y2K bug ... and felt just a teensy bit disappointed when the clock struck midnight and nothing happened. No societal collapse; just business as usual. Still, just after the turn of the century, Australia did witness two other significant collapses. First was at the 2002 Winter Olympics, when Sydney-born speed skater Steven Bradbury became an unlikely gold medallist after his competitors all collided spectacularly, leaving him the last man standing. Then, a few months later, we waved goodbye to a national airline as Ansett Australia landed its last flight.

There were many more entirely unpredictable noughties moments to come. Political satirists The Chaser unleashed a media storm after sneaking past APEC Summit checkpoints while dressed as Osama bin Laden; ex-crim Chopper Read became an unlikely media star; and Merlin from *Big Brother* asked us to 'Free th refugees'.

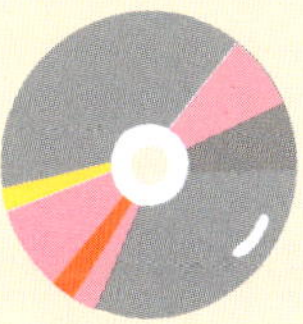

We got a perfect Sydney movie in *Looking for Alibrandi*, a perfect Melbourne TV show in *The Secret Life of Us*, and a perfect sporting moment when John Aloisi scored the penalty that sent the Socceroos to the World Cup for the first time in three decades.

Underbelly became our new obsession, Bec and Lleyton Hewitt our new power couple, and Kevin Rudd our new PM. But the man who started out as our Kevin '07 hero quickly had his shine dulled by that viral video of him swearing like a sailor at his staff, and was ousted by Julia Gillard before his term was through. Oh, and we all got a new go-to retort in 'Not Happy, Jan', care of that inescapable Yellow Pages ad.

DAME EDNA

She was a towering six-foot-something in heels. Her outfits were as loud as her hair, her glasses bejewelled and cat-eyed. And whatever the occasion, she'd greet us the same every time: 'Hello, possums!'

Dame Edna Everage was exceptional in every way. She was an Australian who found equal fame in the US and UK. A housewife turned 'gigastar' (her words) whose public career spanned six decades. A self-described confidante of the royal family ('I've had to change my telephone number several times to stop them ringing me,' she once declared) and a regular guest on celebrity talk shows.

Edna was, of course, the creation and alter ego of comedian Barry Humphries, though we always viewed her as her own woman (and she described Humphries, with the roll of an eye, as her 'manager'). In fact, she was so much her own being that a recurring role in '90s drama *Ally McBeal* was credited to Dame Edna Everage, not Humphries.

For Humphries, it was never about drag, just pitch-perfect performance art and satire, which happened to involve dressing as a woman. He had first created Edna in the 1950s, as a reaction to the prim and proper society standards he saw around him – and despised. 'I invented Edna because I hated her,' he once said. At first, she was Mrs Norm Everage, an *everage* (that's 'average' in the most Australian accent possible) housewife. She evolved throughout the years, becoming a little more fabulous until eventually, as her self-spun story went, she earned a damehood from Gough Whitlam in the '70s. Dame Edna, as she was henceforth known, was the perfect vessel for Humphries to critique celebrity and classism.

Not every show she did was a hit, and outspoken Edna had a habit of ruffling feathers, especially in her later years. But she was a true household name and national treasure, who, in 2007, would even have a Melbourne street – Dame Edna Place – renamed in her honour.

Humphries died, aged 89, in April 2023, taking Edna with him after 68 long years together. We miss them both dearly.

THE SYDNEY 2000 OLYMPIC GAMES

Australia had hosted the Olympics before – the Melbourne games back in 1956. But there was something different about Sydney 2000. Nabbing the Millennium Olympic Games, as it was known, felt like the biggest thing to ever happen Down Under. The event kicked off with a five-hour opening ceremony featuring Aussie icons of all sorts, from surf lifesavers to lawn mowers, dancing box jellyfish and our cuddly Olympic mascots, Millie the echidna, Syd the platypus and Olly the kookaburra. There was also a precocious thirteen-year-old in a pink dress called Nikki Webster, who would soon after regale us with a song about strawberry kisses.

By the end of the Olympics, Australia had won sixteen gold medals – in beach volleyball, archery, cycling and swimming. Ian Thorpe became the hero of the pool, picking up three gold medals for races including the men's 400-metre freestyle. But no victory was bigger than the women's 400 metres on the track. The entire country was watching on 25 September, when 27-year-old Cathy Freeman donned her full green bodysuit and faced off the world's fastest runners. Racing in front of a home crowd of 110,000 (plus another 8.8 million Australians watching on telly), Freeman spectacularly pulled ahead of the pack in the last 100 metres, claiming the gold medal. It has gone down as Australia's greatest ever sporting moment, one made sweeter by its immense significance for First Nations People.

It wasn't just on the sporting field that big things were happening. At a Sydney pub called the Slip Inn, 28-year-old Tasmanian Mary Donaldson was drinking with workmates when she met a Danish bloke called Frederik, who happened to be the country's Crown Prince – not that Mary knew it at the time. A long-distance love bloomed; the pair eventually wed and Mary became our first royal, proving to single women everywhere that you really never know who you might meet during a night out on the town.

KATH & KIM

They were noice, they were different, they were unusual. No two TV characters have made an impact on the Australian psyche quite like Kath Day-Knight and her deadbeat daughter Kim.

They taught us about pash rash, welcome mats, muffin tops and dud roots. In fact, they often blazed their own trail in regard to the English language, whether that pacifically entailed being 'effluent' or 'ferocious readers' (and don't correct Kim on her pronunciation of 'Chardonnay', you pack of chunts).

They were fashion icons, dressed in the best Fountain Gate Shopping Centre had to offer, and always came out looking like hornbags ... even if they did spray-tan the wrong half of their bodies. Together, they so perfectly poked fun at the hopes, dreams and mundanity of Australian suburbia, from Kim's short-lived job in a call centre ('It was really high stress, the amount of abuse on the phone ... that I dished out') through to Kath's habit of smoking one single cigarette each day. (And who could forget their adversaries, Prue and Trude, there to sell you a *throi* for your *courch* with the light roll of an eye.) >

C

In fact, given its colossal impact, it's hard to believe *Kath & Kim* only ran for four seasons (plus a movie). It gave us timeless episodes like Kath's honeymoon, with her great-hunk-of-spunk Kel – which took place entirely at the airport after their mystery flight was cancelled (a GST-related issue, they're told – bloody Howard) and saw them dine at the food court, buy matching Coogi jumpers and try to get into the Qantas lounge by flashing a Video Ezy card. And let's not forget the nuptials themselves, for which Kath stuck velcro dots to her shoes to prevent slipping, and Kim put together a beautiful statue of baby cheeses.

Kath & Kim bottled a type of magic that, as the short-lived US adaptation proved, can't be replicated. So it's no wonder the show attracted a who's who of Australian guest stars across its run – Rove McManus, Dame Edna and the Wiggles among them. The greatest cameos, though, came from Shane Warne (as Wayne, Sharon's Warnie look-a-like beau) and Kylie Minogue, as a pitch-perfect grown-up Epponnee-Rae Kathleen Darlene Charlene Craig on her wedding day. God bless those foxy ladies.

THE 2008 NATIONAL APOLOGY

On 13 February 2008, Australia said sorry. In one of his first acts as prime minister, Kevin Rudd made a formal apology to Aboriginal and Torres Strait Islander People, focusing in particular on the trauma caused by the Stolen Generations.

They were words we'd been waiting for. Bringing Them Home, a report commissioned by the Keating government but only published in 1997 once John Howard had become prime minister, had recommended the Australian government issue a formal apology. But Howard ignored that recommendation, unwilling to use the word 'sorry'.

Rudd pledged to issue the apology if elected – and kept his word. In the House of Representatives, with members of the Stolen Generations in parliament to watch, Rudd was unequivocal in acknowledging the wrongs of so many

previous governments, and the 'profound grief, suffering and loss' caused by the forced removal of Aboriginal and Torres Strait Islander children from their families. To take the first step towards a better future, Rudd said, we had to acknowledge the past. It was a moment that stopped the nation, as we gathered around TV screens to witness formal recognition of the wrong that Australia's governments had done, so First Nations People could take a step forward in their healing. Many First Nations People gathered to watch or listen to the historic moment together – such as in Federation Square in Melbourne – as the prime minister delivered his speech, which was decades in the making and long overdue.

Ian Hamm, one of the Stolen Generation who was taken from his family in 1964, called the apology 'a breakthrough moment'. 'Just to see it, to see the prime minister just spell it out as a fact, a series of facts,' Hamm reflected to the *Guardian* ten years later. 'Not even just about the Stolen Generation, but what happened to Aboriginal people more broadly. And it wasn't an argument, it wasn't a debate, it was just: the sky is blue. The grass is green. This happened, and we need to do something about it.'

STEVE IRWIN

He wore khaki shorts and a permanent grin. Through the thickest of Australian accents, he implored us to 'have a look at the size of this bloke' while approaching a deadly animal of some kind, or perhaps just let out a simple 'Crikey!' He was, as wife Terri once described him, 'like an environmental Tarzan', a larger-than-life figure born to be watched and adored by millions. And adored he was.

But before Steve Irwin became the Crocodile Hunter – star of a show that aired in over 130 countries and reached an audience of 500 million – he was just a guy from Queensland who loved animals. His parents ran a reptile and fauna park, where he claimed to have wrestled his first croc at age nine (and, honestly, we believe him). In 1991 he took over the management of his parents' park and, soon after, met a visiting American tourist there. The couple wed eight months later and spent their honeymoon trapping crocodiles together in Far North Queensland, filming as they went – these home movies eventually becoming the first episode of the reality show that would make him famous. Not long after *The Crocodile Hunter* first hit screens, Steve and Terri renamed the reptile park Australia Zoo, continually improving and expanding it while becoming global superstars.

But, as natural as he was in front of the cameras, Irwin wasn't in it for the fame. As he told it, all he really cared about was the conservation of animals. 'What good is a gold-plated dunny to me? Absolutely no good at all,' he once declared in an interview. 'Every single cent I get goes straight into conservation.'

Irwin routinely put himself in daring situations with animals, both at the zoo and while filming his TV shows. On 4 September 2006, aged just 44, he met his match, pierced in the chest by a stingray while filming on the Great Barrier Reef. A public memorial service was held at his favourite place in the world, the 'Crocoseum' (its official name) at Australia Zoo; it was broadcast live and watched by an audience of over 300 million. Since his passing, Irwin's wife, Terri, and kids, Bindi and Robert (Bob), have carried on his conservation work, but as the days go by we only seem to love, miss and appreciate the big guy more. Strewth, it hurts.

HEATH LEDGER

The turn of the century belonged to Heath Ledger. In 1999, as the millennium loomed, the boy from Perth had his Hollywood dreams sealed by starring roles in two very different hit movies, released within months of each other.

First was teen flick *10 Things I Hate About You*. Ledger was an unknown eighteen-year-old when he showed up to audition for the role of the bad-boy love interest. At that point, director Gil Junger had sat through 'probably 250' auditions looking for the right guy, he later told *The Huffington Post*. 'As soon as Heath walked in, I just felt, "That is a fucking movie star." And it wasn't because of the way he looked. It was just the vibe.' Ledger's innate star quality also scored him the lead role in homegrown flick *Two Hands*, in which he played Jimmy, a spruiker at a Kings Cross strip club who unleashes mayhem when he loses $10,000 of his underworld boss's money.

Between the two roles, Ledger was immediately shot into the stratosphere. It wasn't only his talent or his looks that made him a star, but that harder-to-pin-down, impossible-to-imitate charisma. He was just someone you wanted to watch and intuitively liked. It was, as his *10 Things* director put it, his *vibe*.

Ledger would go on to star in a string of international hits throughout the noughties, from *Monster's Ball* to *Lords of Dogtown* and, of course, *Brokeback Mountain*. The world was at his feet after filming wrapped on *The Dark Knight*, the movie in which he arguably gave his most sensational performance – but then it all ended abruptly. You probably still remember where you were in 2008 when you found out Ledger had died, aged 28, from an accidental overdose of prescription medications. He remains one of our greatest losses.

COREY WORTHINGTON'S HOUSE PARTY

Corey Worthington's parents were on holiday in the Gold Coast when he posted an open invitation for a house party on MySpace. More than 500 people showed up ... followed shortly thereafter by the cops and, before long, the team from *A Current Affair*.

Outraged at the mayhem the sixteen-year-old had brought into a once-sleepy suburban street, *ACA* subjected Worthington to rapid-fire questioning. But their target was unrepentant and unfazed. Shirtless, rocking a pair of yellow sunnies and sporting a nipple ring, he shrugged off everything they could hit him with. What was he thinking? 'I wasn't really,' Worthington answered. Did his parents say he could have a party? 'Er, no.' What do his parents have to say now? He wasn't sure, because every time they called he simply didn't answer. The presenter repeatedly asked Worthington to take off his sunnies, which he refused. ('Nah, I'll leave them on. I like them.')

Just when you thought the interview couldn't get any better, it ended with the most perfect moment. Baying one last time for his blood, the presenter asked Worthington what he'd say to other teenagers thinking of hosting a party while their parents were out of town. 'Get me to do it for you,' he answered without missing a beat. With that, his infamy was assured.

KIDS WANT
CLIMATE
JUSTICE
CLEAN UP YOUR MESS

S

The Avo Toast Tens

There was one food every Australian was eating in the 2010s: macarons. As the new decade dawned, those brightly coloured Parisian sweets became all the rage, spurred in no small part by pâtissier and television presenter Adriano Zumbo. Then there was one food only *one* Australian was eating: in 2015, then PM Tony Abbott was filmed biting into a whole brown onion, skin and all, immediately birthing a billion memes.

In sports, we cheered as Cadel Evans became the first Australian to win the Tour de France ... and were horrified as Australia's cricket team became embroiled in the Sandpapergate scandal. On the AFL field, Sydney Swans player Adam Goodes bravely spoke out about racism within the league, which catalysed a broader discussion of racism in Australia. On the radio, Gotye and Kimbra created one of the most successful Antipodean songs of all time in 'Somebody That I Used to Know'.

And at the movies we got *Animal Kingdom,* a film about a Melbourne crime family that would become a global hit and revive the career of Ben Mendelsohn – who until recently had been paying his bills by working at Brumby's Bakery. He would go on to become a Marvel megastar. His finest line in that flick: 'You haven't been talking to the cops have you, mate?'

In signs of some big steps forward for Australian society, schoolkids went on strike to protest climate change and triple j moved the date of their Hottest 100 from 26 January. And, in a sign of a possible return to the Neanderthal era, everyone started drinking beer out of shoes, a quintessentially Australian and surely very unhygienic move dubbed the 'shoey'.

MICHELLE PAYNE

Michelle Payne was the longest of shots when she saddled up for the 2015 Melbourne Cup. Only the fourth female jockey to ever compete in the race, and riding a horse that had been purchased on the cheap, she was given odds at 101-1. Many are probably still licking their wounds over that decision.

Riding Prince of Penzance, Payne won the race, becoming the first (and still the only) female jockey to ever claim the Melbourne Cup. It was a personal dream realised for the thirty-year-old. Payne, who was raised as one of ten children by a single dad after her mother died in a car accident, had always wanted to be a jockey. She'd even declared at age seven that she would one day win the race that stops the nation. As her career took off, Payne kept her family close. Her brother, Stevie, who has Down's syndrome, was Payne's strapper for the race – a job that includes duties like helping his little sis saddle up. He'd told her before the gates opened, 'Don't get beat. I've got my money on you.' So after she won, the first thing Payne did was jump off her horse and give Stevie the world's biggest bear hug.

But her victory was also a galvanising moment for women around the country, who got to watch Payne eclipse the all-male competition. The fact that she'd smashed that glass ceiling while dressed in the colours of the suffragette movement – purple, green and white – only made her victory sweeter.

So when it came time for Payne to step up on stage, she pulled no punches about the industry she'd had to fight to get to the top of. She described racing as a 'chauvinistic sport' and rather brilliantly told everyone who tried to squeeze her out of it over the years to 'get stuffed'. Her words echoed around the country: 'They think women aren't strong enough, but we just beat the world.' We may have complicated feelings about the Cup itself, but Payne's victory was a moment to celebrate.

JULIA GILLARD'S MISOGYNY SPEECH

From the moment she stepped into the top job, Julia Gillard had dealt with grotesque sexism at every turn, not least from the opposition leader at the time. Tony Abbott had stood in front of placards describing her as a 'witch' and said her government should 'die of shame' – a phrasing that felt pointed given shock jock Alan Jones had recently suggested, only weeks after Gillard's father's death, that he had 'died of shame' because of her 'lies'. Then, one day in 2012, our first female prime minister fought back.

'I will not be lectured about sexism and misogyny by this man. I will not,' Julia Gillard began in her now famous speech, those words met with loud jeers from the men in the room. But across fifteen minutes, calmly, firmly and systematically, Gillard destroyed Tony Abbott, calling him out for his description of abortion as 'the easy way out' and his comments about 'what the housewives of Australia need to understand as they do the ironing'. The noise from other MPs never quite let up, but Gillard didn't falter once. 'The government is not dying of shame, my father did not die of shame, what the Opposition should be ashamed of is his performance in this parliament and the sexism he brings with it,' she fired back. By the time she was through, Abbott's face had gone from a smug smirk to a slumped expression of defeat.

Remarkably, the misogyny speech wasn't pre-orchestrated by a team of speech writers. It just 'welled up', Gillard later described, and she scribbled down points on a sheet of paper before rising to annihilate a man who, as one YouTube comment notes, seemingly aged a year each time the camera panned back to him.

Gillard had no sense, she said, of how the speech would reverberate outside the walls of parliament. But over the coming days, it became a global news story, lighting a fire under millions at a moment when women were allowing themselves to be angry. The speech is still doing the rounds today – it was recorded as a song, 'Not Now, Not Ever', and frequently gets stitched by lip-synching TikTokers.

NOT
NOW
NOT
EVER
!!!

SIA

It's half platinum blonde, half black, with a fringe long enough that it covers almost her entire face. It has become her signature 'do' – in fact, you probably haven't seen a photo of her *without* it for a decade now – but the wig wasn't always part of Sia's look.

Adelaide expat Sia Furler began releasing music in the late '90s. By 2011, she was five albums deep and fed up with the ancillary aspects of being a popstar. She hated being recognised in public, she was sick of touring, and she didn't want to have to deal with other people picking apart her appearance. She decided to retire from being a recording artist altogether, choosing to instead focus on writing songs for other people. But when a song she penned called 'Titanium' made its way to electronic megastar David Guetta, he kept Sia's original demo vocals on the song – without her permission – and released it as a single. It became a runaway hit and Sia was pulled back onto the airwaves.

Sia relented and made another album, *1000 Forms of Fear*, but this time around she did it in disguise. In the video for lead single 'Chandelier', child dancer Maddie Ziegler stood in for her. In performances, press pics and at awards shows, Sia donned the wig. For the few years prior, she'd been hiding her face in photoshoots by putting a brown paper bag over her head, so, really, this was a stylistic level up. But the point was the same: Sia didn't want you to see her face, she just wanted to make music. Now, she has written songs for the world's biggest pop stars – Rihanna, Beyoncé, Katy Perry and Adele among them – as well as sharing many more hits of her own. Her songs have been streamed billions of times, making her arguably one of Australia's most successful artists.

But she still couldn't give a fat rats about being famous. She does, however, like donating the money she makes from her songs to causes like Black Lives Matter bail funds, Haiti earthquake relief and Covid support. And, in an utterly unique donation, every year she gives away $100,000 to her favourite contestant on that year's season of *Survivor* ... just because. So not only is Sia a musical great and noted philanthropist, she's also a reality TV tragic. What a woman.

YES TO MARRIAGE EQUALITY

On 15 November 2017, confetti erupted around Australia. After decades of campaigning for rights by the LGBTIQA+ community, many years of advocacy by marriage equality campaigners and a tortured few months of national debate, the country said yes to marriage equality.

Many of us gathered in parks and city centres to nervously await the result of the survey, erupting into cheers and hugging whoever was closest as it was announced. We danced, we cried and we waved our rainbow flags. Some immediately dropped a knee, pulling out the ring they'd been hiding in their pocket in the hope of a yes result. Together, we bathed in the all-too-rare warm glow that comes from seeing people pull together. It was pure joy.

This step towards marriage equality had been determined by a national postal survey – which, unlike a referendum, was voluntary and the outcome was not legally binding – but almost 80 per cent of the country had participated, with 61.6 per cent voting in support of same-sex marriage. Subsequently, Prime Minister Malcolm Turnbull pledged to have marriage equality legal by Christmas, and on 9 December, the amendment to the Marriage Act passed through the senate. At long last, the right to marry was available to all couples, regardless of the person's sex or gender. Of course, the road that got us there wasn't cause for celebration. The queer community had to wonder why the government couldn't just make the change to the law without first subjecting them to a national debate on their existence and the validity of their relationships. But through all the heartache, we got it done and overwhelmingly agreed that love is love.

In the first six months of marriage equality, more than 3000 same-sex couples tied the knot. By 2020, just before the pandemic came along and ruined the party, that number had swelled to 14,000, as Australians around the country quickly learned that there's no wedding like a queer wedding.

LOVE

LOVE

DAILY NEWS
MILLENNIALS CHOOSE BETWEEN FIRST HOME OR SMASHED AVO TOAST
Xim ventibus etur remqui berit volescia sitates simint aceribus esto maio doluptam litatum voluptas sum que quia esseque etur, solupta pro everspe llac cumquam, velenHarciam assum fuga. Ullupta quident maio dolu
Xim ventibus etur remqui berit volescia sitates simint aceribus esto maio doluptam litatum voluptas sum que quia esseque etur, solupta pro everspe llac cumquam, velenHarciam assum fuga. Ullupta quident maio dolu
Breakfast Menu
Avocado Smash – Small mortgage

AVO TOAST

It started as a breakfast and became a symbol of generational divide. You take some toast (preferably sourdough) and avocado (probably smashed) and garnish it with lemon juice, salt and pepper. Poached eggs optional; extra toppings like dukkah, chilli oil or feta greatly welcomed.

Today, you'd be hard pressed to find a morning menu that doesn't feature avo toast. Alongside our high-quality coffee, the dish has made Australian cafe culture a global export (even New Yorkers will line up for the chance to eat at one of the city's expat-run 'Australian cafes'). We have, in large part, Bill Granger to thank for our national breakfast. In 1993, Granger was preparing to open a new cafe, called Bills, in inner-city Sydney. Council zoning laws prevented the establishment from trading at night, so to bring in a little extra business Granger decided to open for breakfast as well as lunch. Avo toast was on the menu and, seven years later, when he published his first cookbook, he included the dish. Granger probably wasn't the first to ever put an avocado on toast, but he might have been the first to put it on a cafe menu. He was certainly the guy who popularised it. And, before long, copycats of the dish had spread far and wide.

You would think the mildly flavoured, widely loved dish was pretty inoffensive. But, two decades on, avo toast started a generational war. First, in 2016 a columnist at *The Australian* suggested that the millennials' penchant for ordering $22 avocado toast was the reason young people couldn't save a house deposit (that columnist later claimed he was joking, but the nerve had already been struck). The next year a millionaire property developer doubled down and blamed our avo toast *and* our lattes for Australians' inability to get on the housing ladder. Of course, neither was true – forgoing a few Saturday brunches wouldn't do much to make up for those pesky structural issues around housing market growth and wage stagnation. So we kept eating that delicious avo toast – as an act of protest, of course.

HANNAH GADSBY

Hannah Gadsby was meant to be announcing their retirement from comedy with *Nanette*. Instead, the show made them a star.

Gadsby had been on the comedy circuit for more than a decade by the time they put out *Nanette*. They'd done the festivals, popped up on shows like *Rove Live* and *Spicks and Specks*, and found a following with their deadpan humour on the cult Australian TV show *Please Like Me*. And they were over it.

To say goodbye, Gadsby wrote a very different comedy show – one that stirred anger and sadness as much as laughter. In *Nanette*, Gadsby pulled apart the price of existing as a minority in a man's world and reflected on the toll that growing up surrounded by homophobia and hatred had taken on them. They said they were sick of making themselves the butt of their own jokes, explaining that it came at the cost of their own humanity. It was a blistering 69 minutes that reimagined what a comedy show can be and stuck with all who watched it long after the credits rolled.

It was also a runaway success. *Nanette* swept the comedy festival awards and was a critical darling, earning a rare 100 per cent fresh rating on review aggregator Rotten Tomatoes and making Gadsby a global star. Those retirement plans were shelved and Gadsby returned to comedy, making two more comedy specials for Netflix – a little more feel-good than the one that preceded it – as well as penning a *New York Times* bestselling memoir. And when Gadsby publicly revealed their autism diagnosis, many others, particularly women, were encouraged to speak up about their own adult diagnosis of autism, and how life-changing it had been.

All of it proved that sometimes, when you speak your truth, it will resonate in ways you can't even comprehend. May those retirement plans long be deferred.

FINE DINING, AUSTRALIAN STYLE

Australian cuisine can mean a lot of things. It's dimmies and hot chips with chicken salt, purchased from the neighbourhood chook shop. It's a democracy sausage on Election Day, chased with whatever looks good at the baked goods stall. It's chicken parmis, or parmas, and getting in stupid fights on the internet about the correct spelling (it's parmi, you animal).

It's yum cha on a Saturday morning, whether that's washed down with jasmine tea or the less traditional can of Coke (yum cha: hangover edition). It's a chicken schnitzel and avo sushi hand roll, a steaming bowl of pho, a big fat green curry, Halal snack packs and the one specific baklava you drive ten suburbs over to buy (worth it).

It's bush foods like pepperberry and finger limes, embraced by chefs around Australia in the 2010s and now found in many home kitchens. It's fish and chips at the beach, a lamo at Nan's place, picking up a 'bachelor's handbag' on the way home from work, and a Woolies mud cake when Mum couldn't be bothered to bake the real thing. And it's shooing away an ibis or seagull as you dine al fresco. Every bloody time.

SANITISER
2
love
W
BAD

20s

The Stay Inside Twenties

The start of the 2020s may have been dominated by the Covid pandemic, but that was far from the only big story to hit Australia in the first half of the new decade. We watched as terrible bushfires and floods devastated different corners of Australia, prompting comedian Celeste Barber to step in and raise $51 million for relief efforts.

Confined to their couches, parents and kids alike became obsessed with *Bluey*, an ABC kids show about a Blue Heeler puppy that reached a global audience.

Nonbinary Aussies got a new champion in musician G Flip; activist Grace Tame inspired us all; and we cheered on Baker Boy, a rapper from Arnhem Land who won a bevy of ARIA Awards for rhymes woven partly in Yolngu language. On the tennis court and off, Nick Kyrgios leaned into his bad-boy-of-tennis reputation, becoming an anti-hero for the ages.

And we all became *intimately* acquainted with sourdough starter.

THE MATILDAS

When the FIFA Women's World Cup kicked off in 2023, the Matildas were loved by a small but loyal contingent of soccer fans. But by the time the competition was done, it seemed that every last Australian was obsessed with our women's team. People who'd never willingly watched a game of any kind of sport in their life – let alone soccer – suddenly knew who Mackenzie Arnold, Mary Fowler, Hayley Raso and Caitlin Foord were. Even if we didn't understand what being offside meant, we were all deeply invested in the state of Sam Kerr's calf.

Matildas mania built gradually over the early weeks of the World Cup but reached fever pitch in the quarter final, as the Matildas prepared to face off against France. The French squad were favourites to win and the game excruciatingly reached the end of extra time without a single goal scored by either team. So began the longest penalty shootout in the history of the World Cup. It took ten kicks per side to decide the winner, each one watched through fingers, with gritted teeth and a heart rate that would probably concern your cardiologist. When Cortnee Vine scored the goal that snagged Australia victory, the screams were deafening. It was a moment of national unity and celebration.

Existing events around the country were cancelled as Australia prepared for the semi-final against England, which we filled out pubs and parks to watch. There were 11.5 million who tuned in to that game, making it the most watched television program – sport or otherwise – since the current ratings system was established in 2001. We didn't win that one, but it didn't really matter. The Tillies had taught us how to love (soccer ... and each other) and ushered in a seismic shift in how we view women's sports in the process. They were now our pride and joy, the Socceroos lovingly demoted to 'the male Matildas'. Bring on FIFA 2027.

11
18
16
20

COVID LOCKDOWNS

It was the worst of times, it was the weirdest of times. On 11 March 2020, the World Health Organization declared the novel coronavirus a global pandemic and by the end of the month the country was in lockdown. We'd stay there – on and off – for the next year and a half.

The initial rush of excitement that came from Tom Hanks being one of the country's first Covid cases, while filming in Queensland, quickly gave way to misery and malaise. Suddenly, we were separated from families and friends who lived over a state border ... particularly if that state border was WA, which slammed the door shut and enjoyed the perks of its geographic isolation. Towns like Tweed Heads and Byron Bay found themselves

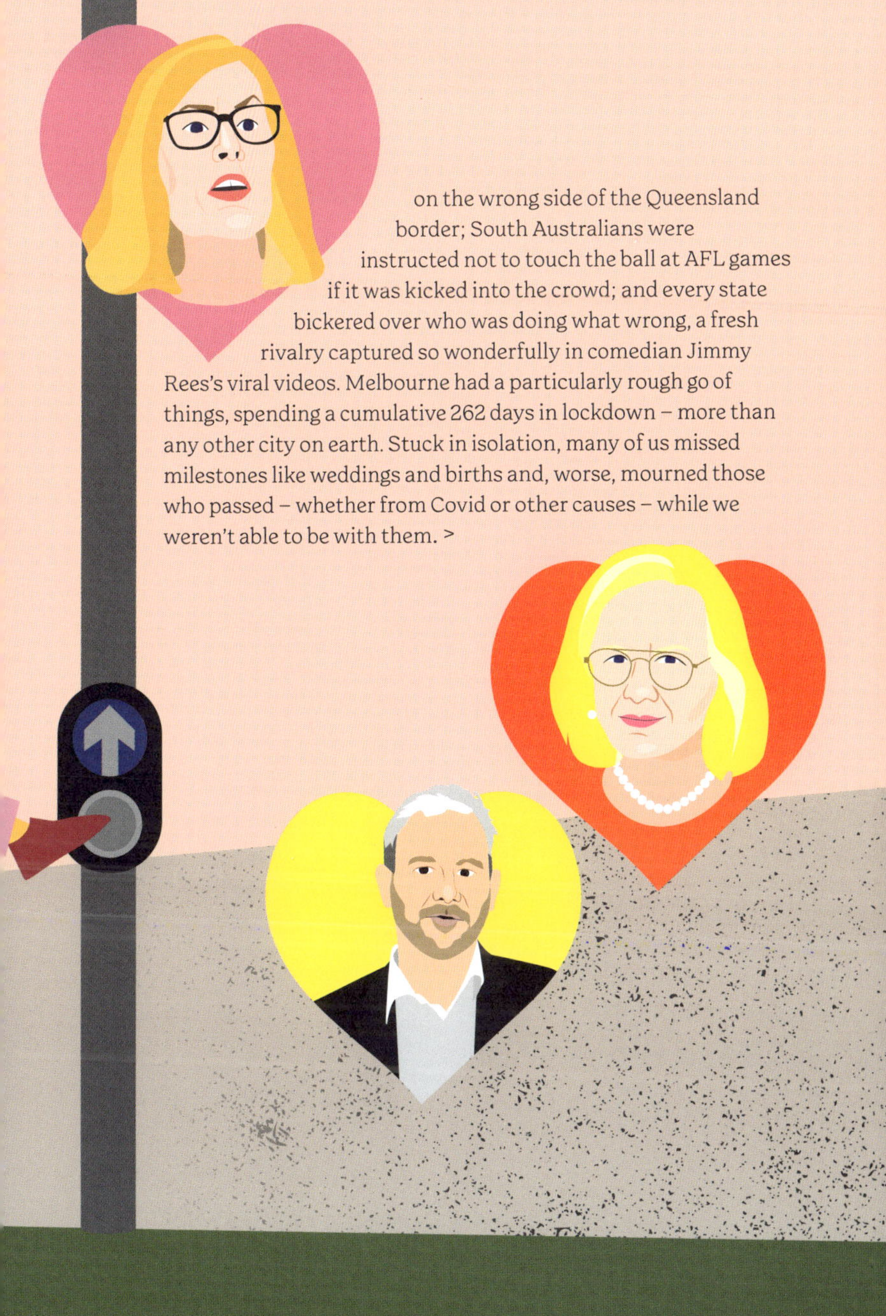

on the wrong side of the Queensland border; South Australians were instructed not to touch the ball at AFL games if it was kicked into the crowd; and every state bickered over who was doing what wrong, a fresh rivalry captured so wonderfully in comedian Jimmy Rees's viral videos. Melbourne had a particularly rough go of things, spending a cumulative 262 days in lockdown – more than any other city on earth. Stuck in isolation, many of us missed milestones like weddings and births and, worse, mourned those who passed – whether from Covid or other causes – while we weren't able to be with them. >

Confined to our homes, we navigated the brave new world of WFH and tried to convince ourselves that Zoom trivia nights were fun (they were not). We began to contend with the horrors of mask-ne (the acne you get under your face mask), went on our silly little mental health walks and formed parasocial relationships with the chief medical officers who suddenly became celebrities (here's to you, Kerry Chant and Brett Sutton), as we tuned in to the morning press conference to hear that day's case numbers. We battled it out at the supermarket for toilet paper, which suddenly became a luxury item ... taking care to stay 1.5 metres away from other shoppers at all times, of course. And, in a sign of our collective insanity, a song that remixed a soundbite of Victorian premier Dan Andrews declaring that it was not appropriate to 'have all your mates around to your house to "get on the beers"' during lockdown came in at number 12 on the triple j Hottest 100.

The spicy cough (as Australia uniquely nicknamed it) eventually receded enough for us to re-enter society, which we tentatively did. Having forgotten all our social skills and now horrified at the prospect of suddenly having to wear a bra again, many of us decided it was easier to just stay on the couch.

DYLAN ALCOTT

At the 2008 Beijing Paralympics, a high-school student from Melbourne set a world record. As part of the Australian men's wheelchair basketball team, 17-year-old Dylan Alcott became the youngest wheelchair gold medallist in the world. For some, such an achievement would have been the pinnacle of their career. For Alcott, it was just the beginning.

In fact, basketball wasn't even Alcott's sport of choice. His first love had been tennis, so a few years later he picked up the racquet again and swiftly dominated that game, too. In 2021, he became only the third professional tennis player to ever claim the coveted Golden Slam, an honour that requires winning singles titles in the Australian Open, French Open, Wimbledon, US Open and the Paralympics all in the same calendar year. Proving there's a little Shane Warne in us all, he downed a tinnie from his champion's trophy at the US Open to celebrate.

But sports isn't Alcott's only passion. He also loves music and has always been a devoted festival-goer, where he has a habit of wheelchair crowd-surfing. A photo of him riding atop a sea of heads in his wheelchair at one such event went viral, catching the eye of triple j, who gave him a job as a presenter. So a couple of years later, it only made sense that Alcott started Australia's first fully inclusive and accessible music festival, Ability Fest. He'd go on to be named 2022 Australian of the Year, the first person with a visible disability to claim the honour in the prize's 62-year history.

Life wasn't always smooth sailing for Alcott. He's spoken openly about how he struggled with depression as a teenager, taunted by bullies for being in a wheelchair. Everything changed, Alcott said, when he found a lifeline through sport and became proud of his disability. Alcott retired from sports after claiming that Golden Slam and now focuses on advocating for disabled young Australians through The Dylan Alcott Foundation, so they can have the same opportunities he's had. 'Being a good tennis player is not the priority of my life,' he said of his decision to bid farewell to professional sport. 'Being a good person is.' Legend.

MARGOT ROBBIE

It's a great Australian tradition to launch an acting career on *Neighbours* – but few have done so as successfully as Margot Robbie. At age seventeen, after a job making sandwiches at Subway, the Gold Coast girl moved down to Melbourne to take up a role playing Ramsay Street regular Donna Freedman. For a while, she was a standard Aussie soap star, who'd rock up to the Logies in a mullet-shaped dress (short and poofy up the front, long down the back), party all night, then clock in to set the next day, battling a ferocious hangover.

But before long the bright lights of La La Land started beckoning. A couple of years after taking a chance and moving to America, Robbie nabbed her breakthrough role in Martin Scorsese's *The Wolf of Wall Street*, starring opposite Leonardo DiCaprio. Her star power was obvious and from there it was hit after hit: *Suicide Squad*; *I, Tonya*; *Once Upon a Time in Hollywood;* and *Bombshell*– and Robbie swiftly became one of Hollywood's most in-demand actors.

Her biggest role came in 2023 when she so perfectly played Barbie, a beautiful and beloved doll in the grips of an existential crisis. Of course, Robbie didn't just act in that blockbuster movie – she made the whole thing happen. Robbie bought the rights to the film from Mattel, pitched it to studio Warner Bros, convinced Greta Gerwig to direct and only stepped into the title role after Gal Gadot declined the offer. Her hard work paid off – *Barbie* broke box-office records, raking in more than $1.4 billion worldwide; its poetic evisceration of life under the patriarchy resonating with women everywhere. But then in a life-imitates-art turn of events, neither Robbie nor Gerwig, the two women in charge, scored Oscar nominations for their work on the feminist flick. The Academy may not have given Margot the nod, but she'll always be our Best Actress.

TONES AND I

She started out as a busker and went on to release one of the most successful Australian songs ever. It's hard not to be inspired by the story of Tones and I, aka Toni Watson. Trying to get noticed in music the best way she could think of, Watson moved from her home in Melbourne's Mornington Peninsula to Byron Bay, to live out of her van and start performing for passers-by on the street.

Incredibly, the very first time she set up her keyboard in that northern NSW town, a music manager saw her and was struck by her talent. He slipped her his business card, they began talking and six months later he offered Watson the bush cabin out the back of his Gold Coast hinterland home. She could stay there to write music, he offered. And she did. There, Watson penned a song called 'Dance Monkey', which was inspired by time she'd spent busking in Byron, dealing with the often drunk crowds who'd treat her like a monkey performing for their entertainment – stealing her earnings, trying to play her keyboard and booing her when she packed up for the night.

The song became a runaway hit. 'Dance Monkey' hit number one in over 30 countries worldwide, including here in Australia, where it became the longest running number one single ever, beating a record previously set by Bing Crosby in the 1940s. It became the most Shazammed song of all time and the most streamed song on Spotify by a female artist – more than anything made by Beyoncé, Rihanna or Taylor Swift.

But Watson is modest about her success. 'I loathe that song a lot of the time,' she told the radio station Nova FM, explaining that at this point, she's a little tired of singing it, which is fair enough. But, hey, three billion streams (and counting) can't be wrong.

ASH BARTY

Ash Barty was known for being composed on court: a tennis star as humble as she was unflappable. But on 29 January 2022, after the shot that claimed the Australian Open, Barty let out an uncharacteristic roar. The crowd, who had been pin-drop silent just a moment before, erupted into wild cheers. For the first time in 44 years, one of our own had won the women's singles crown.

Barty's success in the early stages of the Australian Open had united both hardened tennis fans and those who didn't know a backhand from a serve, all of us joining the 'Barty party' and desperate for the girl from Ipswich to go all the way. And, with the country watching, she did – 4.21 million people tuned in to see the 25-year-old win in straight sets against American Danielle Collins, making it one of the most viewed Australian sporting events of the last two decades.

And the feel-good moments didn't end there. Barty, a proud Ngarigo woman, had long been mentored by Australian tennis great Evonne Goolagong Cawley, a Wiradjuri woman who herself had claimed the Australian Open title in the 1970s. Their bond was a special one, but Goolagong Cawley had been unwell in the lead-up to the final and told Barty she wouldn't be able to attend. At the last minute, not wanting to miss the moment, the tennis legend secretly snuck into the arena. When it came time for the trophy presentation, the announcer declared that there was a 'special guest' here to handle the honours, and Goolagong Cawley strolled onto the court. The look of joy and surprise on Barty's face was priceless. Just as we were basking in the rare wonder of seeing one First Nations female sporting great present the trophy to another, the camera panned to the crowd in the stands ... where Cathy Freeman was watching it all unfold. The ever-gracious Barty used her speech to thank her family, her team and everyone involved in the match, right down to the ball kids.

Only a few months after the Australian Open, ranked as World Number 1, Barty announced her retirement, telling us she had 'given absolutely everything I can to this beautiful sport'. What a way to go out.

How Far We've Come

Australia has come a long way since the 1950s. We've gone from watching black-and-white variety shows to making movies that are exported around the globe. We've developed our own strain of slang, whether that means hitting the bottle-o, drinking savvy b, dealing with mozzies, chucking a sickie or evasively answering 'yeah, nah'. We've raised sporting heroes and beaten the English at their own game more times than we can count. We've made important changes in how we treat First Nations People and culture, from banning walking on Uluṟu to always knowing whose land we're on. We've had prime ministers good and bad, embraced local bush foods as well as flavours from around the globe, and learned to celebrate our wins with, as Kath and Kim taught us, 'BBQ Shapes and a bottle of Baileys'. We don't yet know what the future holds, but our hope is that, through all the turmoil and change, she'll be right.

ABOUT BECK

Beck Feiner is an illustrator and author. Her art and stories shine a light on social issues and tap into the mood of the time to promote harmony and diversity. Beck has created many much-loved picture books, including *Aussie Legends Alphabet*, *If I Was Prime Minister*, *The Polar Bear in Sydney Harbour* and *Big Love*, which received a CBCA Notable Award.

Beck's formative years were spent working out what cost more: the jacuzzi or the jetski on *The Price is Right*. She only recently learnt that *Picnic at Hanging Rock* was not a true story, and is thinking about starting a petition to bring back mint Paddle Pops. She also highly recommends using something longer lasting than icing to cover the naked torso of the Barbie for *The Australian Women's Weekly* Dolly Varden cake.

ABOUT KATIE

Katie Cunningham is a freelance writer working primarily for *Guardian Australia* where she covers culture and lifestyle, and writes the weekly column 'Three Things'. Her work has also appeared in a range of publications including *The Sydney Morning Herald*, *Crikey*, *VICE*, *The Big Issue*, *frankie* and *Rolling Stone* magazines.

Katie's first crush was Ricky Ponting. She had *The Australian Women's Weekly* Barbie cake for both her 7th and 30th birthdays, and a photo of Ben Mendelsohn in the 1996 comedy/thriller *Idiot Box* was her phone screensaver for about five years.

ACKNOWLEDGEMENTS

From Beck

Strewth! I got to work with a dream team on this project. A massive thank you to Melissa Kayser who helped me bring this idea to life and with whom I share a love of Aussie kitsch outfits. Also to Katie Cunningham for writing with such perceptive humour about Aussie culture and always entertaining my late night emails like 'We forgot the shoey!' And to Virginia Birch, Kristy Allen and Erika Budiman for your editing and design superpowers.

Thank you to my agent, Tara Wynne from Curtis Brown, for all your support and wisdom over the years. To Jill Large, for your Aussie expertise and ongoing grammatical support. To my parents, for letting me watch quite a lot of TV and thus helping me to become so knowledgeable in the area.

And lastly to my kids, Esme and Levi. I know I have to *ask* you to read my books but I hope you read this one and learn valuable information, like what a 'bachelor's handbag' is, and that it takes people from many diverse backgrounds to make this country wonderful. I love you both to the moon and back.

You Beauty!

From Katie

A huge thank you to Beck Feiner, Melissa Kayser and Virginia Birch for trusting me with this project – what a dream it's been! And an extra thanks to Beck for being so easy and so much fun to work with. Your emails will always make me laugh.

The National Film and Sound Archive was an invaluable resource while researching this book, and truly made me appreciate how important funding our national archives is. Thank you to Shanks for your moral support and vital discussions on the most iconic *Kath & Kim* moments. Thank you to Jared Richards for the author solidarity and reassuring voice notes. Thank you to my parents, especially my dad, who served as my unofficial boomer correspondent throughout the writing process. And thank you to Luke Smith for being the best, most supportive partner imaginable. I will always take every possible opportunity to tell you how much I love you.

Published in 2024 by Murdoch Books,
an imprint of Allen & Unwin

Murdoch Books Australia
Cammeraygal Country
83 Alexander Street
Crows Nest NSW 2065
Phone: +61 (0)2 8425 0100
murdochbooks.com.au
info@murdochbooks.com.au

Murdoch Books UK
Ormond House
26–27 Boswell Street
London WC1N 3JZ
Phone: +44 (0) 20 8785 5995
murdochbooks.co.uk
info@murdochbooks.co.uk

For corporate orders and custom publishing, contact our business development team at salesenquiries@murdochbooks.com.au

Publisher: Melissa Kayser
Editorial manager: Virginia Birch
Design manager: Kristy Allen
Designer: Erika Budiman
Editor: Emma Schwarcz
Illustrator: Beck Feiner
Production director: Lou Playfair

Murdoch Books acknowledges the Traditional Owners of the Country on which we live and work. We pay our respects to all Aboriginal and Torres Strait Islander Elders, past and present.

ISBN 978 1 76150 052 7

A catalogue record for this book is available from the National Library of Australia

A catalogue record for this book is available from the British Library

Colour reproduction by Splitting Image Colour Studio Pty Ltd, Wantirna, Victoria
Printed by 1010 Printing International Limited, China

10 9 8 7 6 5 4 3 2 1